500 Tips for Communicating with the Public

by the same authors

Once Upon a Group
A Guide to Running and Participating in Successful Groups
2nd edition
Maggie Kindred and Michael Kindred
ISBN 978 1 84905 166 8

A Practical Guide to Working with Reluctant Clients in Health and Social Care
Maggie Kindred
Illustrated by Cath Kindred
ISBN 978 1 84905 102 6

of related interest

Effective Communication
A Workbook for Social Care Workers
Suzan Collins
ISBN 978 1 84310 927 3
Knowledge and Skills for Social Care Workers series

Communication Skills for Working with Children
A Guide to Successful Practice Using Social Pedagogy
3rd edition
Pat Petrie
ISBN 978 1 84905 137 8

Working with Children and Young People Using Solution Focused Approaches
Establishing Respectful and Effective Communication
Judith Milner and Jackie Bateman
ISBN 978 1 84905 082 1

Recording Skills in Safeguarding Adults
Best Practice and Evidential Requirements
Jacki Pritchard with Simon Leslie
ISBN 978 1 84905 112 5

Best Practice in Professional Supervision
A Guide for the Helping Professions
Allyson Davys and Liz Beddoe
ISBN 978 1 84310 995 2

Supporting Relationships and Friendships
A Workbook for Social Care Workers
Suzan Collins
ISBN 978 1 85905 072 2
Knowledge and Skills for Social Care Workers series

500
Tips for
Communicating
with the
Public

Maggie Kindred and Michael Kindred

Jessica Kingsley *Publishers*
London and Philadelphia

First published in 2011
by Jessica Kingsley Publishers
116 Pentonville Road
London N1 9JB, UK
and
400 Market Street, Suite 400
Philadelphia, PA 19106, USA

www.jkp.com

Library of Congress Cataloging in Publication Data
Kindred, Maggie, 1940-
 500 tips for communicating with the public / Maggie Kindred and Michael Kindred.
  p. cm.
 ISBN 978-1-84905-175-0 (alk. paper)
 1. Communication. 2. Oral communication. 3. Business communication.
4. Social interaction. I. Kindred, Michael, 1937- II. Title. III. Title:
Five hundred tips for communicating with the public.
 P90.K467 2011
 153.6--dc22

                          2010046397

British Library Cataloguing in Publication Data
A CIP catalogue record for this book is available from the British Library

ISBN 978 1 84905 175 0

Printed and bound in Great Britain

To all clients, colleagues, experts and friends who have helped us to write this book.

Acknowledgements

Thank you, Malcolm Goldsmith, for being a co-author for the original version.

Thank you, colleagues at Jessica Kingsley Publishers, for your tactful and helpful support.

As this is not an academic book, we have not acknowledged in the text the many experts who have helped us with our practice over the last 40 years or so. The omission of names in the text is because so much of the material has become part of us through constant application and adaptation; hence we cannot attribute it accurately. This could present you with a problem – especially if you do not agree with anything, or need to refer to our sources – so we would be very pleased to hear from anyone who would like to engage with us.

Overall, we would like you to see the book as the sum of our experience rather than our academic knowledge. It represents what we have learned from *others* who are good communicators.

Contents

INTRODUCTION   11

Why do we need to communicate well?   11
Tips about the tips!   12
Book structure   12

1. How Do We Communicate? 15
Communicating verbally – face to face   15
Communicating verbally – giving presentations 19
Communicating verbally – on the telephone   21
Non-verbal communication – writing   23
Non-verbal communication – electronic written
    communication   26
Non-verbal communication – body language   30
Non-verbal communication – communicating
    imaginatively!   33
Different modes of communication –
    communicating one to one   35
Different modes of communication –
    communicating with groups   37

2. Skills for Communication......... 45

Listening skills	45
Questioning skills	47
Assertiveness skills	49
Information-giving skills	52
Advice-giving skills	53
Reassurance	55
Disclosure	57
Challenging	57
Negotiation skills	59
Dismantling barriers	61

3. Emotions in Communication...... 65

Clients and workers have feelings!	65
Angry feelings – conflict management	69
Handling stress	74
Using humour	75

4. Communication in Different Settings....................... 77

Where to meet?	77

5. Structured Communication....... 81

Preparing yourself first	81
Scene-setting	82
Preparing the location	83
Setting the tone	86
Introductions	87
Relationship length	89
Setting goals	90
Handling interruptions	91
Summarizing	92
Endings	93

6. Communicating with Different People 97
    Working with men and women   97
    Working with children   98
    Working with people of different races and cultures 100
    Working with clients who do not speak English   104
    Working with disabled and differently-abled people   106
    Working with older people   108
    Working with people of different sexualities   110
    Wealth, class and society   112

7. Communicating with Self-awareness 115
    Know yourself   115
    Personal bias and agendas   119
    Making judgements   120
    Think about your expectations   122
    Using labels   122

8. Professional Boundaries and Responsibilities. 125
    Boundaries   125
    Confidentiality   128
    Being clear about roles and responsibilities   130
    Communicating in the workplace   131

9. Rights, Advocacy and Meeting Clients' Needs. 135
    Meeting needs   135
    Understanding rights   136
    Helping your client to make decisions and choices   138
    Being an advocate   140

10. Communication and Procedures . . 143

Know the rules   143
Assessment   145
Recording and reporting   147
Background checks and safeguarding   148
Dealing with abuse   150
Responding to complaints   151
Supervision   153
Reflecting on practice and developing your
    communication   154
Appraisal   156

EPILOGUE   159

Introduction

This book contains advice for all who work with people – at 'the front line' – and in particular those who work with clients in the helping professions.

Why do we need to communicate well?

People have always tried to communicate from the minute they were born, and perhaps take for granted their ability to do so effectively. However, communication does evolve, having grown more sophisticated and complex as societies have developed.

Within the 'helping professions', in which communication is central to the job, some pioneers decided that they needed acquired skills as well as natural ability, and started to draw upon the ideas and skills found in training for counsellors: the development and analysis of different kinds of language, both verbal and non-verbal.

Communicating with the public is not counselling the public, but we believe that volunteers, carers, public servants and everyone in the helping professions can benefit enormously from learning adapted forms of counselling and communication skills.

Tips about the tips!

On the subject of learning new skills, when one of us was learning to play golf, a friend would say from time to time, as a wind-up, 'Now remember the 1001 pieces of advice I've given you before you hit the ball!' Although this was a joke, it was a reminder that learning a new skill or ability can be overwhelming if considered in that way. We don't want these 500 tips to be daunting, so tackle them in bite-sized chunks.

We have used the word 'client' generally throughout the book, as it seems the most generic word for recipients of public services. However, much of the advice can be extended to cover any other person with whom you have a professional relationship – be they client, service user or colleague.

For the most part, we hope that the advice within this book will help you to do your job more effectively, but it comes with a health warning: some bad habits may have to be ditched!

Book structure

Communication is a vast and complex subject, and does not break down neatly into self-contained sections. However, when compiling the advice within this book we have attempted to start with the basics and then progress to some of the complexities and tensions that are often encountered by professionals when dealing with the public, particularly those in people-centred professions.

First, we look at what communication is – the many ways in which we communicate the skills involved in communicating well. Then, we consider some of the decisions that professionals need to make about how to communicate – how to handle emotions, where the communication should take place and how to structure communication. Next, we offer some guidance on the challenges and rewards that are involved in working with diverse groups of clients and the importance of being aware not only of the preferences and needs of others, but also your own. Finally, the book addresses communication issues particular to those working in a professional setting – how to balance professional boundaries and responsibilities and yet still have a strong rapport with your client.

Our aim in writing this book is not just to guide the reader, but also to provoke them; it's not possible within the confines of a book to tell you how to communicate well in every situation and you may not remember the 500 pieces of advice, but it is hoped your 'swing' will improve!

Chapter 1

How Do We Communicate?

Communication uses channels – a million different kinds, including body language, words, images and signs – and takes many forms. It can be a conversation between two people, a group discussion, an argument… Here are some tips about the basics of communication.

- **As a starter exercise, list the different types of communication you can think of in order to understand and improve your use of them.**

Communicating verbally – face to face

- **A vital starter: 'Get your brain into gear before opening your mouth'.**

- **Be aware of the limits of the spoken word.**
  Spoken communication is likely to be the first response when prompted to list forms of communication, but be aware of its limitations. It's commonly stated that over

90 per cent of the communication of attitudes and feelings is conveyed not verbally but through non-verbal means.

- **Words, once spoken, are difficult to take back.**
  Words are unlike letters in their immediacy – when you write a letter, compose a text or type an email you can edit it before sending. So the spoken word is a spontaneous and powerful too, but can also be dangerous.

- **Control your tone of voice and emphasis.**
  The tone in which you speak can radically alter the meaning of what you are communicating, particularly when combined with non-verbal facial expressions.

- **Try not to butt in while your client is talking.**
  The best kind of conversation is two-way, with neither person dominating it. Of course, this may be difficult with someone who is very talkative, and you may have to find a kind way of getting a word in edgeways.

- **Recognize your vocal style.**
  Listen carefully to other people's speech. Is it, for example, clipped, relaxed, officious, reassuring, judgemental, furtive or attractive? What about the rhythm? Is it disjointed, making it hard to follow what is being said, or flowing and easy on the ear? Does the intonation help to maintain interest, or is the delivery very flat and likely to make the mind wander? Is there adequate stress on important words or phrases?

- **Try to avoid using jargon.**

  Jargon is a word that describes terms used by specialist professionals or academics as a shorthand to communicate complex ideas. Examples might include 'predictors of beaconicity', 'taxonomy', 'level playing field', 're-baselining', 'benchmarking', 'seedbed', 'slippage', 'mainstreaming', 'holistic', 'contestability' and 'synergies'. In reality, they can obscure the meaning of what is being said.

- **Conversely, clichéd words and phrases can be communication aids.**

  You may not like phrases such as 'go with the flow' or 'blue sky thinking', but they actually unite people by being almost universally understood. So it is helpful not to dismiss any platitude or cliché your client may use. Having said that, take care not to introduce jargon through your own communication; avoid using words and phrases which can patronize people – present yourself as a human being, not a bureaucrat.

- **When conversing with a client, try to avoid correcting his or her language.**

  For example, if he or she describes the midday meal as 'dinner', don't change it to 'lunch' when you respond. Pages 113–114 touch on class and language – remember that the language a person uses can reflect a part of their identity.

- **Take care in dealing with a person whose accent is not easy to understand.**

  Embarrassing situations can arise if each person is constantly having to say to the other: 'I'm sorry,

I didn't catch that', 'Pardon' or 'Would you mind repeating that', whether the communication is face to face or over the phone. If at all possible, try to find out beforehand whether or not the person with whom you will be dealing originates from an area of your own country which has a strong accent or speaks English as a second language. If you have an accent yourself, it can be helpful to mention it.

- **Be aware that even if someone understands you speaking, he or she may not necessarily be able to answer.**
  Some people may be able to understand spoken or written English well, even though they have difficulty in speaking or writing in English themselves. This is another of the ways in which people do not fit neatly into boxes.

- **Remember that there are huge differences in the way the same words are used or interpreted.**
  This does not only apply to different races, but also to social classes and even regions. Learn the local version!

- **Try to avoid using 'we' inappropriately, especially early on in a client relationship.**
  When we say, for example, 'We know that…' or 'We'll try this approach', this assumes that the person opposite is in agreement…they may not be! 'We' can mean 'you and I', 'our organization' or 'one' (the so-called 'royal we'), so when you use the word be sure that you know what you mean, and, more importantly, that the client knows what you mean.

- **Words associated with politeness and good manners vary from culture to culture.**
  For example, in many Asian languages, the words for 'please' and 'thank you' are not normally used except on very formal occasions.

- **Remember that language is a living thing.**
  It is not static. If you look at a dictionary from, say, a hundred years ago, how many words in it have now fallen into disuse, and how many new words have since come into being? Keep yourself as up to date as possible with current words, phrases and idioms so that you are able to respond appropriately when they come into a conversation.

  Finally, in this context, the following little-known adage is worth committing to memory:

  The kindest word in all the world is the unkind word, unsaid. (Anon.)

Communicating verbally – giving presentations

- **Giving a presentation is less intimate and less interactive, but still a very effective way of communicating.**

- **Prepare for your presentation.**
  You may have to present aspects of your work to colleagues, clients or outside bodies as part of your job. As with everything, preparation is all (we recommend referring to the material on preparation covered on pages 81–82).

- **Some important preparation points.**
  Decide on your main points: no more than three in a ten-minute talk. Is there a logical connection between these points? What evidence can you produce to support your points and make your case clear? Prepare your visuals: PowerPoint slides, overhead projector foils, etc. Make sure they are clear, and that any text is big enough (24 point or larger).

- **The presentation itself will be less frightening if you:**
  1. briefly introduce yourself
  2. check that your audience members can all see and hear you
  3. let people know if you are going to take questions as you proceed or invite discussion at the end, and
  4. give an outline of the structure of the talk, so the audience knows where it is going.

- **Lead the audience through your main points in a logical and interesting fashion.**
  Where they are appropriate, you could plan to use anecdotes, slides, video clips, charts, graphs and case histories.

- **Decide when to give out handouts before the presentation.**
  If you have handouts, will you issue them at the start, in the middle or at the end?
    Summarize what you have said and make your conclusions clearly.

- **Plan to leave the audience with a parting shot to stimulate their thoughts.**

Communicating verbally – on the telephone

- **Telephones allow people to communicate with emotion, conveying warmth or urgency in our voices, and to forge some kind of bond through conversation.**

  However, over half of the non-verbal tools for establishing rapport are lacking. There are now technologies, such as Skype, which enable computer users to communicate both verbally and visually. These represent a small fraction of overall phone use at present, but this will no doubt change in the coming months and years.

- **Don't forget about tone of voice when using the phone.**

  Perhaps even more so than in face-to-face contact given the lack of accompanying visual expressions, your voice will be the quality that assures the caller that you are happy and willing to help them or solve their problem.

- **Use a consistent greeting every time you answer the phone.**

  Formulaic business-style responses can be off-putting, so if you are setting up a standard response within a department, give careful thought to how it will sound to the person contacting you. The standard format is often something like: 'This is Anytown Social Services, Winston speaking. How may I help?'

- **Put people on hold, but don't desert them.**
  If you have to put people on hold, do it in a way that assures them that they have not been disconnected or forgotten about. Remember always to ask for a caller's permission to place them on hold and wait for their response before doing so. The same applies when transferring a call to someone else.

- **People tend to think of the phone as a tool of urgency and recognize its therapeutic value.**
  As all crisis and advice helpline organizers know, it is a simple, convenient and effective way for someone to seek advice, perhaps anonymously, and is a much more immediate and nuanced form of communication than emails or text messages.

- **Leave clear answerphone messages.**

- **Think out what you want to say beforehand.**
  Write it down if need be. This helps to avoid 'ums and ahs', and the accompanying trailing off of the voice, while you rack your brains. Bear in mind that most answerphones have a message time limit.

- **Wait for the beep to finish before speaking.**
  This is so obvious, but it's worth a reminder. When you are very busy you can easily launch in too soon.

- **Start with your name and your organization if you belong to one.**
  Again, when under pressure you may be so concerned to get the message across that you forget the obvious.

- **Speak slowly and distinctly.**
  When you leave a message, be aware that some answerphones don't record as clearly as you might expect. Be careful when pronouncing certain letters. For example, 's' and 'f' are easily confused. Also, if your accent is not the same as the recipient's extra clarity is required.

- **If you leave a phone number, email address or postal address, repeat it.**
  Do this at a slower pace than the rest of the message.

Non-verbal communication – writing

- **Remember that everything written is double strength.**
  This is particularly important when an unpleasant message has to be given, such as informing someone about a death.

- **Never write anything which you would not like to read if addressed to yourself.**
  This is about how things are written, taking on board the point about everything put in writing being stronger. For example, 'I NEED IT NOW!!!' makes a manager's case but is horrible for the staff member to read. Gentle language is much better. Try to translate what has been said about clipped and curt (versus tactful and kind) speech into your writing or typing.

- **Bear in mind that written communication is not accompanied by softening non-verbal communication.**

  In email correspondence 'emoticons' are sometimes used as a substitute for non-verbal facial expressions but cannot offer nuanced communication. An emoticon is computer-speak for small images or symbols which represent the writer's mood or facial expression. A simple example is :-), or ☺, which is made by pressing the following keys: colon, hyphen, then close-bracket.

- **Conversely, writing can be a way of expressing yourself without the social pressure associated with face-to-face communication.**

  It can be freeing not to be constrained by feelings about one's own appearance. This must have huge positive benefits for those who are sensitive about how they look, an equal opportunities contribution applicable to many states and conditions.

- **In a professional context, accuracy does matter.**

  Pay attention to grammar, spelling and handwriting or typing. There is nothing wrong with asking a colleague to proofread for you. Some people would say these aspects matter just as much in a non-professional context!

- **Make sure you match your writing style to the reader.**

  Everyone has their own personal style, but it is worth considering how an appointment letter to a teenager might differ from a request to the Director.

- **Write with structure.**
  This risks seeming like a boring reminder of being taught essay writing at school, but it is important for achieving the desired end, whether you are writing a letter, report, memo or email. No-one wants to read something long and rambling; on the other hand, it needs to cover everything it is meant to.

- **Consider the kinds of fonts and formatting you use.**
  The use of bold for the tips is for emphasis, but note that they shout, as do CAPITALS, and large letters.

- **If you receive something unpleasant from someone else in writing, try to suspend negative judgements about it.**
  It is your behaviour you have control of, not that of your clients or colleagues. Write a neutral response offering to discuss the matter face to face as soon as possible. Given the comments about the power of the written word, it is wise to avoid detailed responses.

- **Don't be dismissive about forms and administration.**
  Much writing in professional contexts is not drafting carefully worded letters or essays, but filling in administrative forms or assessments. Much maligned, forms can actually be an excellent communication tool. It's worth focusing on the fact that they are not just a tedious means to the end of gaining a resource or information, but can enable you to find out important things about the client through an impersonal medium. They can be used to help structure communication,

provide information about the client and his or her preferences, and, if filled in by the client, can give him or her a chance to communicate in a different way.

- **Use forms wisely.**
  It's important to use forms appropriately, and at the right time. If you are using a form as part of a structured interview with a client, it could either be introduced at the beginning, as a pro-forma for your session, or at the end.

- **Remember that dealing with anything to do with numbers and calculations can be a problem for some people.**
  If you need to discuss anything involving this aspect of communication, try to be aware of any difficulties the client may have and revise your approach accordingly.

Non-verbal communication – electronic written communication

- **Be wary of the immediacy of emails.**
  You may argue that this is the same as all written communication, but the difference is that emails are often drafted hurriedly, at the speed of spoken language, but with none of the time to reflect. Pause before pressing the send key!

- **Respect privacy.**
  Electronic communication makes it very easy to send large amounts of data to lots of people in an instant. Take care to follow rules regarding data protection,

read email 'strings' before you send them on, and respect the privacy of private correspondence.

- **Mind your own business.**
  Looking at someone else's emails is the same as reading their letters or going through their drawers. In a professional context, it may be entirely appropriate and time-saving to do so, but there needs to be a code of conduct about such matters.

- **Have a good grasp of 'netiquette'.**
  A lot of people have grown up using electronic communication instinctively, but do not necessarily know their 'netiquette' any more than they know their grammar. Some basic rules include: always include a subject line and make sure it is appropriate to your message; always include your name (not including it is like making a phone call without giving your name); and don't forward chain letters and hoaxes.

- **Learn at least some of the language.**
  At risk of contradicting what has already been said about correct grammar and respectful style, in a world where real-life facial expressions and vocal intonations are impossible, abbreviations and symbols become almost necessary for written expression online. Some common examples which you will be familiar with are as follows: Please = pls; four/for = 4; LOL = laugh out loud.

- **Be clear about why you are emailing.**
  Before you send the email, consider what you are asking for – re-read the email to check that this is

clear – include important information where it can be read clearly.

- **Write in a focused way.**
  Experiment with trying to include one subject per email. This can help to keep your message clear and to the point.

- **Be aware of the possibilities and pitfalls of communicating on social networking sites and chat rooms.**
  There are huge potential advantages to using social networking sites such as Twitter or Facebook to bring people together. Such sites provide a forum for individuals to test each other out without the risks inherent in personal contact, which is why chat rooms and online counselling are so popular among people who find it hard to form relationships. However, when making sensitive communications online it is worth asking the question: 'Would/should/could I say this face to face?'

- **Recognize the potential of electronic communication for clients with particular needs.**
  Spell-checks can be a great help to people with learning difficulties such as dyslexia, while people with disabilities can participate in online communities and 'virtual worlds' without any of the social stigma that commonly exists in society.

- **Be discriminating about information or advice you find on the Internet.**

  The Internet can be a rich source of information and resources that you can draw on when communicating with clients, whether it be guidance on issues that concern them or ideas for working with them. Always check that your source is reputable and read the material thoroughly before communicating it to your client.

- **Use of computers may alienate some clients.**

  Problems can arise, for example, if technology fails at a critical moment, or if their computer skills are limited. This book has been written assuming that the reader regularly uses a computer, but not everybody does. Always make available other methods of getting in touch, especially if you have not heard from someone when expected.

- **Know the dangers of disclosing personal information.**

  If you are assisting your client in using the Internet, ensure he or she is aware of the risks involved in disclosing personal details online; this might be through taking part in competitions, communicating in chat rooms or responding to emails asking for information. This is particularly important when working with children and young people or vulnerable adults.

Non-verbal communication – body language

- **Understand that most face-to-face communication is non-verbal.**
  Unconscious non-verbal messages often reveal more than the spoken word in conveying true feelings and attitudes. They might be visible in the way you stand in relation to a client, or whether you look at them directly.

- **First of all, practise watching how people behave as this could help you in your work.**
  Try to find situations where you can watch people's behaviour unobtrusively – you mustn't be accused of spying! For example, when queuing, waiting in a public place, shopping or watching live television you have the chance to observe people in many different situations and to gain insight into all kinds of verbal and non-verbal behaviour.

- **Realize the potential of non-verbal communication.**
  Non-verbal communication can also be conscious and include many more elements than 'sign language'. The tips that follow offer some examples of this.

- **Recognize that behaviour is communication.**
  Shaking hands, offering open arms and even exhibiting unpleasant behaviours such as stamping your feet or screaming are examples of ways in which people's behaviour acts as a form of communication. Even withdrawal – *not* communicating – can be a way

to send a message to the person with whom you are communicating.

- **Understand why someone behaves as they do.**
  People who use their behaviour, rather than language or facial expressions, to communicate may be unable to express feelings or choices; they may not have the capability to use facial expressions or speech or communication aids. Alternatively, they may have tried communicating but feel like they are not noticed or listened to.

- **Monitor your facial messages.**
  The face is a powerful tool for communication and is perhaps the most obvious way to communicate non-verbally. It can be a conscious or unconscious way of showing that you feel sad, angry, concerned or happy. Take care to avoid communicating feelings that you do not wish to communicate.

- **Mind your hand language!**
  Self-touching actions, such as touching the face, scratching, gripping the hands together or putting the hands in or near the mouth, can communicate signs of tension or stress.

- **What do your behavioural tics communicate?**
  The classic phrase 'talk with your hands' can be helpful in some situations, but not when you are drumming on the desk, which usually indicates boredom or irritation.

- **Remember that in every social situation there are approved and inappropriate postures.**

  For example, consider a situation where a professional sits down in front of a client, crosses arms and legs, or reclines back, and begins the session. The client is unlikely to want to respond, because those positions are either unreceptive or too casual. Assertive behaviour – gently leaning forward or sitting in a way that reflects the client's own posture – can be a useful starting point.

- **Don't sit facing each other directly as this can feel very confrontational.**

  Place the chairs at a slight angle to each other.

- **Maintain a discreet personal space where possible when working with clients.**

  Naturally this will change depending on the context, but generally speaking, about 4–12 feet (around 1–3 metres). Many people will feel uncomfortable if you do not do this, though be aware that there are cultural variations.

- **Appreciate that people from different races and cultures use facial expressions to communicate in different ways.**

  Eye contact during verbal communication is expected in the UK because it implies attention and respect toward others. Within Asian culture, eye contact is considered as the opposite, particularly to women, those in authority and older people.

Non-verbal communication – communicating imaginatively!

- **Think laterally about what forms of communication you could use with your client** – there are many tricks and tools out there that you can put to use!

- **A picture can be worth a thousand words.**
  Even though you, like a lot of people, may not jump to drawing as your first choice of communication, be open to the idea of using images. Many people are inhibited by the fact that they are not artists, but most of us connect immediately to a diagram or sketch, and they are immediate ways in which both client and worker can communicate information.

- **Use drawings, logos and symbols.**
  All of these can be used as a simple way to communicate messages. Give thought to the images you use. This is not a question of artistic ability; drawing stick figures can be a simple but direct way of communicating ideas.

- **Cut pictures from magazines.**
  This needs preparation – if the images are portraying people, ensure there are positive representations of people from diverse backgrounds available for the client to choose.

- **Use real-life accessories.**
  For example, showing someone a kitchen utensil they have not used before is much better than describing it.

- **Appeal to the senses.**
  Think how you can utilize the five senses: sight, sound, smell, touch and taste. People with learning disabilities and dementia benefit greatly from this type of environment, so scented plants, soft fabrics, evocative pictures, provision of healthy drinks and music are all helpful.

- **Consider using sign language.**
  There are many forms – Makaton is an internationally recognized communication programme used by people with various forms of learning and speech difficulty in more than 40 countries worldwide. British Sign Language (BSL) is the first or preferred language of deaf people in the UK. It makes use of space and involves movement of the hands, body, face and head. The Braille system is a method that is widely used by blind people to read and write. It is different from sign language, since it relies on touch as its communicator. These days, many people with visual disabilities use audio; this means that they are using Braille less, although there is still some demand for documents in this format.

- **Experiment with ecomaps.**
  Ecomaps were originally conceived as a diagrammatical representation of a person or family's interactions with other individuals or groups in the community, but can be adapted to suit all kinds of purposes. Put a keyword or drawing in the centre of a big piece of paper and place smaller related symbols or words around it. They can be connected by lines or colour-coded, and their importance can be represented by their size or distance from the centre – be creative!

- **The construction of an ecomap is a simple task which can lead to a complex response.**
  It can be a very powerful process and may raise a number of varying emotions within those completing the work. For example, a child may suddenly give the name of a previous foster sibling the worker did not even know about. The social worker needs to be mindful of this and to be sensitive to the emotions of the subject.

- **Make visual materials age-appropriate.**
  For example, do not give children's pictures to an adult.

Different modes of communication – communicating one to one

- **Be aware of the relative strengths of one-to-one communication as opposed to communication with a group.**

- **One-to-one communication is the most intensive and common form of communication.**
  It is the obvious and natural form, so not much thought is given to it in everyday life. Professionals sometimes need training to overcome some common unhelpful practices they have grown up with.

- **Communicating on a one-to-one basis has the advantage of privacy.**
  This is particularly important where strong feelings are involved, and for confidentiality.

- **One-to-one communication is best in short bursts.**
  Take breaks when you or your client needs them. No session should be longer than an hour – even this is three times the 20-minute attention span commonly recommended by educationalists.

- **Be aware of the disadvantages of a private conversation.**
  If communicating with several individuals about the same subject, you may inadvertently give slightly different messages about the same topic to different people. It can also be more difficult to corroborate what has been discussed.

- **One-to-one communication allows for providing tailor-made advice.**
  Even though a *tête-à-tête* is more time-consuming than groupwork, it provides an excellent opportunity for the worker to provide guidance that is tailor-made for that person.

- **A worker can focus solely on the client's problems and needs in a one-to-one situation.**
  One of the disadvantages of groupwork is that the leader has to juggle with multiple relationships and this involves trying to be equally attentive to each member's difficulties and requirements.

  It is usually a lot easier to make an appointment to see one person than it is to get several people together in one place at one time.

- **One-to-one communication can provide a greater feeling of job satisfaction for the worker.** All of his or her efforts are concentrated on one individual, and although the intensity of this may have its downside in that the worker and/or the client may feel under pressure, there may be a worthwhile harvest!

Different modes of communication – communicating with groups

- **Working in a group can be a more efficient, time-economic and enjoyable way of working with clients.**

- **There is nothing mystical about 'groupwork'.** Communicating with groups is often described as 'groupwork', which can make it sound like it requires expertise to engage in. However, it's likely that you'll be doing groupwork every day as part of your regular job, even if it's small informal group meetings.

- **Groups can bring together as much knowledge and skill as there are people in the group – and more!** There is a relevant saying that 'a group is more than the sum of its parts', and this is presumably because group members stimulate each other to reveal skills and knowledge that they did not know they had.

- **If clients have something in common, they can benefit from the contributions of their peers.**
  This is the principle behind support groups for people with a particular condition, or who are carers, for example.

- **Groups add a new dimension to the dynamics of communication.**
  As the number of members who are relating to one another increases, so too does the complexity of communication. In a group of three people, A, B and C, there are three pairs of relationships going on. Add one more person and the number of relationships doubles. In a group of eight people, there are 28 pairs of relationships to be managed! It can be a fine balance between 'many hands make light work' and 'too many cooks spoil the broth'.

- **Groups present the opportunity for carrying out activities or playing games.**
  Group activities or games can be useful icebreakers, can facilitate communication, and are a useful way of getting people to talk about themselves and with others in a more relaxed atmosphere.

- **Know the common styles of behaviour in task-centred groups.**
  - ▸ **Activism.**
    Getting the job done, making sure your own part in the process is fulfilled properly, not wasting time on seemingly irrelevant discussion.

▸ **Proposing.**
Initiating ideas, suggestions, courses of action relevant to the task.

▸ **Seeking information.**
Asking for facts, opinions or clarification from other members of the group.

▸ **Giving information.**
Offering facts, opinions or clarification concerning the task.

▸ **Encouraging.**
Being warm, friendly or supportive of others by verbal and non-verbal means.

▸ **Gatekeeping.**
Lowering barriers by positively attempting to involve others in any activity concerning the task or the maintenance of relationships. Making barriers by excluding, cutting off or frustrating others in any activity concerning the task or the maintenance of relationships.

▸ **Harmonizing.**
Being prepared to compromise and actively accommodate others in order to preserve harmony in the group.

• **Know your own style.**
Which of the above do you recognize in yourself?

- **A healthy group needs a balance of all the functions.**
  If yours does not, try printing the list out and having a discussion about it in the group. People can change their behaviour!

- **To facilitate group communication you need to be organized and make sure your own part in the process is clear.**
  It is very easy to duplicate effort, so time spent in communication with group members to ensure everyone knows exactly where they are at all times will reap ample rewards. The more you meet with the same group, the easier this will become.

- **Consider whether or not you need an outside facilitator.**
  Doing so has the advantage of freeing up team members to play a full part in the team, but the facilitator needs time to get to know the team properly and may have to be paid. Is there anyone in your training department who could do this work for your team?

- **Be aware that you may need to mediate the communication of others in a group setting.**
  It can be more of a challenge to steer discussion and to avoid group members being offended in a group setting; for example, if someone makes a remark about something being 'gay', the person next to them who happens to be gay could react with hostility or withdraw from communication.

- **Understand the difference between a group and a team.**
  They share many characteristics, but teams are usually all working towards a unified goal.

- **Identify opportunities where you can 'team-build'.**
  Teamwork doesn't just happen with colleagues – you can also team-build with your clients – for example if working with families and carers. This can bear much fruit all round, as those relatives and other helpers who feel secure in their relationships with staff may be more likely to give more of their time and effort in working as a team.

- **There are more ramifications to confidentiality when you are working as a team.**
  You need to agree when particular information is released to individual clients, because great ill-feeling follows if word gets round informally and some clients feel excluded.

- **Be aware that some aspects of the service you provide can actually stand or fall by your ability to work as part of a team.**
  If you have followed media reports of enquiries into tragic service failures in child protection, you may have noted that breakdowns in team communication are always cited.

- **Groups and teams make numerous decisions –
  realize how you are making them.**
  Often that is what they exist to do, so it is worth
  thinking about the *processes* of decision making,
  which generally just happen – or don't! Who has a
  say, and does any particular individual make a final
  decision? Some decisions will be stronger if arrived at
  collaboratively, others – perhaps a decision that needs
  to be made in a rush – benefit from being made by
  one person.

- **Consulting is different from collaborating.**
  Consultation is often mistakenly thought of as a
  democratic process. People like to feel that their view
  is being heard and that they are making a contribution,
  but consultation can go wrong if the decision-maker
  does not make it clear that they will have the final
  word. Clients whose views are ultimately overlooked
  become disillusioned and less ready to put forward
  their views next time. How many times have you heard
  people say, 'What's the point of asking us, the decision
  has already been made'?

- **True consensus is rare but powerful.**
  Courts aim for this from their juries. It is rarely truly
  achieved, in the sense that the minority voices are often
  under pressure to give in because of time constraints
  or subtle bullying. However, it does produce the best
  kind of decision, with maximum commitment from
  all. Consensus can take a very long time to achieve;
  a group must hear all the arguments over and over,
  without putting pressure on anyone, and must try to
  be as rational as possible.

- **Groups and teams have more fun!**
  Of course this is not always true, but the creativity, helping each other along and humour which occur in a well-functioning team or group may leave individual work far behind if the group members can see a common purpose.

- **Work with the family as a group.**
  'Family' is interpreted here in the broadest sense of children living with adults who may or may not be their birth parents. The group does not need to include everyone in the family: three people or more is a group.

- **Family groupwork can be effective in addressing many issues.**
  Working with a family group can help to bring conflicts into the open as a way of beginning to resolve them. It acknowledges that people operate in groups all the time (the family is their first) and that it's worth investing in making this group more effective and comfortable. It also allocates time to people in a cost-effective way, and it can demonstrate new ways of handling things, or 'modelling', for its participants.

- **Consider family group conferences.**
  In a family group conference (FGC), a parent/aunt/uncle/grandparent gets together with the child or young person and the rest of the family to talk, make plans and decide how to resolve a situation. It is a process usually initiated by a professional, but the professional steps back as the process progresses. The family communicates as a group, rather than each

person communicating individually with each other member which brings the risk of misunderstandings. It falls outside of the scope of this book to do so, but there are a number of really good books out there on how to do FGC well.

- **Generally, aim to be understood, rather than risking being misunderstood.**
  Most of the time, we want to be understood when we talk to, write to, phone or text another person. Language, in all of its various forms, is a tool. Like a tool in a workshop, handle it with care and don't let it go rusty, or else it may not perform the job it's supposed to, and can hurt you and others.

Chapter 2

Skills for Communication

You can acquire communication skills through reading about them in books like this and, most importantly, practice.

Listening skills

- **Adopt an attitude, posture and facial expression which conveys to the other person that you want to hear what they are saying.**
  Attention spans have generally become shorter in recent years. It can be easy to find your attention wandering if there isn't the kind of constant stimulation that you have become used to.

- **Listen 'between the lines'.**
  As important as the actual words are the messages given in delivering them, indicated by the quality of the voice, inflexion, emotional tone, rhythm, the style

of speaking and what words are stressed and how. Add to this the non-verbal messages people give out, and you can see how advanced listening skills can be likened to learning a foreign language.

- **Make a mental note of key words or phrases.**
  Making a conscious mental note can help you to recall what was said in the encounter if you're not taking notes. In conversations, you may notice that a particular word is being repeated from time to time – ask yourself if it has any significance. For example, if a person keeps mentioning one of their relatives, are they giving away how they feel about that person?

- **Make sure that you are hearing what the client has actually said, and not what you want to hear.**
  A lot of processing of what our ears pick up takes place in the brain when we listen to what people are saying. This process can be affected by how we feel about the person and by any prejudices we have.

- **Even if you understand your client perfectly, it does no good if you don't communicate that understanding.**

- **Summarize to show that you are listening and to check that you understand your client's needs and motivations correctly.**
  Sum up what you think you have just heard, for example: 'You seem to be saying that you would like…' The client then has the chance to change any misperceptions on your part.

- **Remember, clients know whether you are listening to them or not by the quality of your response.**
  If you do get caught failing to pay attention or you respond in a way that shows you are not listening, apologize.

- **Use small silences between conversations.**
  These help the listener to reflect, compose his or her response, and create a sense of calm. Don't overdo it – about 3–10 seconds is enough.

- **Assess the quality of the silence.**
  Silence is not neutral – does it feel angry, threatening, sad, reflective, relaxed, encouraging…?

Questioning skills

- **Recognize when questioning is useful.**
  It is useful, for example, when you need precise information, you need to open up an area, or you need to prompt.

- **Know the four main types of question:**
  1. open questions (e.g. 'And then what happened?')
  2. closed questions (e.g. 'Do you prefer tea or coffee?')
  3. leading questions (e.g. 'What annoys you about X?')
  4. probing questions (e.g. 'How do you feel?').

- **Keep your questions short and to the point.**
  Don't string several questions together all in one breath as this can be confusing and can increase the level of anxiety. Encourage your client to avoid this too!

- **Avoid 'why' questions – this is the language of the interrogation room.**
  Those of us who are parents will recognize the tendency, at the end of a long hard day, to scream at a child, 'Why did you do that?' We rarely get a useful answer!

- **Try not to ask too many questions unless you have to.**
  People can think of 'interviewing people' as questioning them, and in some situations gathering information in this way is appropriate. However, when you are trying to assess a situation where someone feels upset, or where their lifestyle is being scrutinized, your client will feel freer if you observe and listen. The client is more likely to open up if he or she is not being interrogated.

- **If your client doesn't respond to a question, avoid simply repeating it.**
  He or she is clearly reluctant or unable to speak about it, and persistent questioning won't change this.

- **Think before you respond to a question from the client.**
  Into which of these categories does it fall?

1. a question seeking information concerned with the subject of the session

2. a personal question which has arisen out of the subject of the session

3. a personal question which has nothing to do with the session

4. a non-personal question which appears not to be relevant to the subject of the session.

- **Respond to questions concisely.**
  Be brief – some clients can be anxious about the interview, and can't readily absorb and process a lot of information. They may switch off quite soon once you have started speaking. When a young girl the authors knew asked a question, she would hurriedly add: 'Can I have the short answer please?'

Assertiveness skills

- **Understand what assertiveness is.**
  Being assertive is essentially about giving clear messages. Here's an unclear message:

  Can I speak to you for a minute? I don't know how to put this, but you upset me the other day, and I feel really upset... the thing is you were very rude, it's a shame because I like you normally...

  The speaker eventually spells out what he or she is upset about. A clearer message would be: 'I think you are very good at... [this must be honest!], but you did not give me a chance to present my case at the staff meeting.' Expressing yourself in an assertive way is the right balance between meek, vague communication on one side, and avoiding bluntness on the other.

- **Understand what assertiveness is not.**
  Some people, when trying to make a point, can come across as overbearing, authoritarian, unkind, never wrong, and even rude. This is not assertiveness!

- **Giving clear messages is important.**
  Your client deserves to be communicated to clearly, even if the news is not pleasant. You may be in a position of giving bad news to someone who already feels vulnerable, or you may be uncomfortable with a decision you have to impart. Avoiding the subject or tiptoeing around it will not help your client.

- **Be assertive when you encounter unacceptable behaviour.**
  Clients may not always realize they are displaying unacceptable behaviour. While you need to be kind and patient, tolerating bad behaviour does the clients no favours – they simply lose the chance to make lasting relationships.

- **Practise saying 'No'.**
  Many people find it a problem to refuse someone anything, and most assertiveness courses feature 'saying no' as a specific part of the programme. Take note of the following saying: 'If you can't say "No", what is your "Yes" worth?'

- **You can use the direct 'No'.**
  When someone asks you to do something you don't want to do, just say 'No'. No apologizing; be direct and succinct. 'No, no thank you.'

- **Or you could use the reflecting 'No'.**
  Here you acknowledge the content and feeling of the request, then you add the assertive refusal at the end: I know you want to hear about the result of the meeting today, but I'm sorry I can't tell you yet.

- **Feedback can be a constructive accompaniment to saying 'No'.**
  Once you have made a decision to refuse your client, it can be helpful to feed back to them why you have done so as it may help them to achieve a more positive response in future.

- **Know how to give feedback well.**
  First, decide what behaviour you would like the other person to change. Be sure that it is something that they can do something about (for example, someone with a speech impediment may struggle to communicate more clearly). Try to give the feedback shortly after the event to avoid storing up feelings; be discreet if possible; and be specific: to be told that 'you are very aggressive' is less helpful than to say 'I thought you shouted at me unfairly just now.'

- **Feed back using the right language.**
  Start sentences with 'I'; for example, 'I would like you to...' This personalizes the communication and helps both parties to 'own' it.

- **Saying 'No' can be difficult to do in practice.**
  It is easy to agree with the above, but it doesn't mean that doing it will be easy; many will always find it difficult to be assertive and say 'No', particularly if faced by an emotional or angry client.

Information-giving skills

- **You are seen as a source of authoritative knowledge.**
  Ensure you familiarize yourself with the specialist knowledge that you will need in working with your client. This might mean checking your organization's literature, visiting your library or carrying out research online (ensure that any research carried out online draws on reliable sources). If leaflets are available, have some to hand in case your client would find it useful to have one to take away.

- **Make sure that any information you give is up to date.**
  Do you know the latest laws, rules and regulations in relation to your field?

- **Tailor information to the needs of your client.**
  Distributing information about products or services to clients and customers is ineffective and can cause frustration if they do not meet the client's requirements. Part of your role will be as a 'filter' to provide him or her with relevant information.

- **Check whether your client prefers information in writing.**
  It's preferable to provide information in writing to avoid it being forgotten or misinterpreted.

- **When communicating information, choose the right time.**
  This is particularly crucial when bad news has to be imparted. For example, you may have to give someone information about planning following a difficult and complicated medical diagnosis.

- **Ensure that you are aware of information supplied by colleagues.**
  You need to ensure clear and consistent messages are communicated to the client.

Advice-giving skills

- **Advice is necessary when guidelines are needed for dealing with a situation or a condition.**
  This relates to the communication of technical information, so is different from telling people what they should or shouldn't do. For instance, doctors have found that meeting patients' expectations for information, explanation or help with decision making leads to better outcomes.

- **Know the limits of advice giving.**
  Advice may not be welcome if it suggests that your client is being judged or if you dictate to them. For example, 'My training tells me that this child is not

developing normally for her age', or, 'You need to let Nila be more independent'. You may be right, but you are unlikely to achieve a warm or cooperative relationship with clients.

- **Advice offered has consequences.**
  In ordinary life, one can become rather casual about offering people 'pearls of wisdom'. You may enjoy telling people what to do in a situation without necessarily thinking of the consequences, but in a professional context you can be responsible for the consequences of your advice. Where possible, all advice should be confirmed to the client in writing but *always* recorded on the client's file.

- **Be prepared before you offer advice.**
  Consider situations that might arise as a consequence of your advice. If you have no time to prepare before meeting a client, try to buy time to think by gently asking further questions, or by offering advice phrased as a question. For example, 'How would you feel about…', or, 'What would you think of…'

- **Only offer reliable advice.**
  Don't rely upon information on the web or which you have been told anecdotally unless you have established that it is trustworthy. Who wrote or provided the information? Are they qualified to write about this subject? Do you trust the organization? What is its purpose? Why did they write it? Assess anything you find on the web for quality and relevance.

- **Make sure you are fully aware of guidance provided by your organization in respect of giving advice.**
  If the nature of your job entails the frequent giving of advice you should have an adequate understanding of these guidelines.

- **There is a difference between giving advice and offering it.**
  If it is vitally important that a person takes your advice but it's not at the level of police or medical intervention – for example the person may need to be stopped from harming him or herself or others – you may strongly advise them, stating that, 'It is absolutely vital that you...'. If the matter is less urgent, you may phrase the same advice as, 'I think you should definitely consider...'

- **Clients are less receptive to advice when feeling threatened or under pressure.**
  Try using a follow-up interview once the person has had a chance to reflect

Reassurance

- **Know what it is to reassure.**
  Reassurance is the act of restoring someone's confidence; it is an action-linked technique, a way of giving people courage to face a problem or to help them know that you support them in pursuing a suitable course of action.

- **Don't reassure when it's not going to be all right.**
  It is generally better to try to understand a person's experience more clearly than to give inappropriate reassurance. If someone has been injured badly, it is only helpful to tell them they will be all right if you are in a position to know that they will be.

- **Know that reassurance can patronize and sideline a client's opinions.**
  If someone is facing loss of independence, for example entering a care home, all the advantages in the world that the new setting offers won't compensate for losing one's home, so don't list them at this point. The act of reassuring can ignore clients' valid concerns and fears.

- **Reassurance is powerful in a crisis.**
  It can be an important part of information giving and can help individuals to regain a feeling of control. For example, in the case of delayed travel, the fact that people are often left with no information by the authorities weighs far heavier than the delay itself.

- **Reassurance can be an emotional tool.**
  If someone is out of control, it may be that they need you to appear especially calm, even if the situation is fraught. A warm smile and a message that all is well with the world can help.

- **Be sparing with compliments – they are closely related to reassurance.**
  If you overuse compliments you run the risk of being patronizing. Try to make them as specific as possible; for example, 'I found that a very helpful description of your circumstances'. Avoid being too general; for example, 'You're doing well'.

Disclosure

- **It can be instinctive to want to disclose details about yourself in order to establish a rapport with your client.**

  It may seem natural to talk about your own problems or experiences – for example if you have experienced similar problems to your client – but think twice before you do so. Your situation is never the same as someone else's; even if you think the circumstances are remarkably similar, the client may disagree. Factors such as your status, your education and your role as a professional can make a difference.

- **Self-disclosure can bring benefits.**

  Sharing a little about yourself when prompted, such as giving information about whether or not you have children if asked, is a friendly and helpful gesture.

- **To disclose or not to disclose?**

  Given that it can be problematic to do so, consider the following questions first: who is going to benefit from me talking about myself? Am I actually wasting precious time by talking about me? Am I avoiding tackling difficult issues? Do I want to be liked? Am I simply tired and hungry and want to go home?

Challenging

- **Learn to challenge constructively.**

  If you do need to challenge someone else's statement or behaviour, try to avoid doing so in a confrontational way. Good challenging should be a way of helping people to accept something they need or to revise their opinion without entering into a 'tug-of-war' with them. It does not mean taking an accusatory stance or being aggressive. In essence, it is getting across a message that the client might not want to hear, or hadn't been aware of. See also tips on giving feedback (page 51) and conflict management (pages 69–73).

- **Some challenges are about discrepancies between how you see a situation and what your client does or says.**
  For example: 'You say you feel fine, but you are near to tears all the time'. It could also be that you interpret a situation differently. If so, this needs to be acknowledged by you verbalizing the two views and both of you examining them.

- **If you challenge your client, the language you use should be clear, assertive and unambiguous.**
  Avoid using vague words to try and soften the situation, such as 'I mean to say...', 'I don't know how to say this but...', 'I hope you won't be upset...' – such language simply delays and obscures. You may use your own feelings as part of this communication; for example, 'When you called Nila a 'Paki' I felt very sad'.

- **Challenges work best when the client feels safe with you.**
  However, if a new client insults you, you may not have the luxury of a pre-existing relationship. You can use reflection as a technique here: 'When you said I was bloody useless, were you telling me how desperate you feel?' Note that reflective comments are usually offered as questions rather than statements – they

don't contradict the client's statement, but do still act as a challenge to the client.

- **Where you can do so, frame challenges positively – relate to the client's currently used and unused strengths rather than their perceived weaknesses or lack of skill.**
  For example: 'You said that you were "thick" but you have ten GCSEs.'

- **Be cautious about challenging someone using written communication.**
  Whether in an email or a letter, communication is more memorable and permanent when recorded – you are more likely to remember written comments by teachers on your school work. So, if you need to challenge your client, do it face to face in a safe setting.

Negotiation skills

- **Know that negotiation is not just for business deals – it is something that people do all the time.**
  For example, people may use it in their social lives for deciding a time to meet, or where to go on a rainy day. In working with the public, it is 'bread and butter'.

- **Negotiating is useful as a conflict-resolving skill.**
  If you and your client cannot agree on a course of action, you can set out what the 'bottom line' is, and ask your client to do the same. For example: 'I will contact the Benefits Agency on your behalf, if you will be honest and tell them how much you really earn in a week', is a negotiation. It is a kind of bargain.

- **It's fine to make appropriate bargains with people.**
  Because negotiation can feel like a transaction, 'helpers' who do not traditionally see themselves as business people can be reluctant to engage. However, negotiation does and should form a part of everyday human communication. Think about parents trying to get their children to eat their dinner using the 'bargaining chip' of dessert.

- **There is nothing wrong with a compromise based on negotiation, so long as this is ethically achieved.**
  Unethical examples are offering favours in return for information, or dishonest flattery.

- **Don't prolong negotiations if you have not been successful.**
  In the helping professions you are not trying to pull off business deals, just improve someone's situation as best you can. The apparently unsuccessful discussion today may bear fruit tomorrow.

- **Know how to try to persuade a client, when negotiation has failed, that an important course of action is needed.**
  Although we have said that you shouldn't prolong negotiations if you haven't been successful, there are times when it is important for the client's well-being, physically or mentally, to do your best to get him or her to agree to your decision about the situation. This is where you need to be kind but firm. As clearly as possible, point out the benefits of agreeing and the

disadvantages of not agreeing. If your job includes the power to enforce a law or regulation, do this in as caring a way as possible.

• **Good negotiating isn't about winning and it isn't about someone else losing.**

Dismantling barriers

• **Barriers to good communication take many forms.**
These can be physical (for example staff located in different buildings or on different sites) or physiological (from individuals' personal discomfort, or caused by ill health, poor eye sight or hearing difficulties), but by far the biggest group of barriers are to do with messages going wrong: poor communication, by any other name.

• **Make a list of the ways in which you think you and others may be erecting barriers.**
This should help you to work as a team to get rid of them.

• **Try to motivate others to help dismantle barriers.**
This can be challenging. You can consider using an incentive, but avoid shifting the responsibility for improvement solely onto others. When two or more people engage in communication, all have responsibilities for making it effective.

- **Learn ways of dismantling the barriers and act on them.**
  Work as a team and find some ways of giving each other honest feedback. Based on what you discover, make plans on how to make changes that will enable you to break down some of the barriers.

- **If working with the public in a community setting you can involve key people and groups from the local community to help build bridges.**
  This can be done to help build bridges both within the community and between clients and professionals. Community education workers can be invited to meet residents to discuss their interests and to run community education classes. Collectively, they often possess the skills to communicate with a much greater range of people than an individual can.

- **Being able to receive feedback is one sign of strength of personality, and being willing to act on it is another.**
  Don't imagine the dismantling of any barriers will happen overnight, and be prepared for some home truths! Feedback may be a bit unpalatable at times, but make an effort to recognize accurate feedback and think about how you can address it in your actions.

- **Treat yourselves each time you feel you have made some significant progress.**
  This might be a form of refreshments or an enjoyable activity – you can plan ahead what these little treats could be.

- **Work with those barriers you can do nothing about.**

  For example, you may have to live with your offices in one building and your resources for clients in another. What does not help is for you to share your own frustration about things like this with the client – it is better to listen to the client's anger, and then say you will do the best you can to provide the service as soon as possible. The same applies to outdated equipment or staff shortages, though it is permissible to tell service users if there has been a temporary emergency, such as everyone struck by a mystery virus, or delayed because of bad weather!

- **Dismantle the most important barrier – people's reluctance to communicate with you.**

  The more you can communicate sincerely to people that you understand their reservations about seeing you, the better your success rate is likely to be.

- **Ensure you have access to a 'safety valve'.**

  Your supervisor needs to know about anything which is getting in the way and take action if necessary; this may include unclear instructions, teamwork problems or your state of mind if it is distracted by private worries or ill health. You are a human being not a robot!

In essence, skills for helping are about attracting, keeping the interest of and, to a certain extent, controlling the client: be kind but firm.

Chapter 3

Emotions in Communication

With all this advice on learned practical skills, it is easy to forget how much your own emotional state, and that of your clients, affects relationships profoundly. This section explores the challenges of understanding feelings and their important role in communication.

Clients and workers have feelings!

- **Be aware that people can be hugely apprehensive about meeting professionals.**
  Coping with strange job titles increases the fearful anticipation. It is particularly important to remember this in any kind of institution, which for the professional is home ground.

- **Check your own emotional state before seeing your client.**
  If you don't you may approach him or her feeling tired, stressed, scared or angry. It is worth spending a little time on improving your state of receptivity. This does not change whatever else is going on in your life one iota, but it can make or break the piece of work you are on now.

- **Take the time to regulate your emotional state.**
  Sit down, close your eyes and remember a time when you felt really confident/happy/refreshed. Picture in your mind what you said, hear what you heard and feel what you felt… Now enhance those images. Make the pictures brighter and bolder, the colours richer, the sounds louder and the feelings stronger. Stay with this recollection for a few minutes, bringing your mind back every time it wanders. You will feel refreshed by the brief rest and mini brain-holiday, so that you begin your session with a client in a more helpful frame of mind.

- **Respond to the emotional client in a calm and reassuring way.**
  This helps to deal with any turmoil he or she may be experiencing.

- **Communicate with emotional intelligence.**
  Don't say, 'Are you all right?' or, 'How do you feel?' when your client seems to be exhibiting symptoms of unease, such as sadness, agitation or anxiety. How can they be all right, when the situation is obviously all wrong? Both responses show a lack of empathy and invite scorn. Instead, a non-verbal response may be appropriate, or perhaps, 'Is there any way I can help?'

- **Be empathetic, but take care when expressing sympathy.**
  For example, you can imagine what it must be like to have no money – empathy. However, if you say so and sympathize with the person, you risk being considered patronizing; your client will see you as a professional with a comfortable job. Likewise, when witnessing a client's anti-social behaviour you may sympathize with their motivations, but it would not be helpful to express this.

- **Be clear about the difference between empathy and sympathy.**
  Sympathy is more akin to pity, the need to give comfort, and express reassurance. These feelings are not wrong, they are human, but may cause people to act hastily to relieve pain. Ask yourself, 'Who am I trying to help here, myself or the client?'

- **Clients recognize real empathy.**
  It has been discovered in counselling practice that trying to hide thoughts and feelings behind a professional mask is not helpful in establishing successful communication, which poses a conundrum for professionals. On the one hand, you cannot express whatever you feel, in whatever way you please; on the other hand, you need to be honest. There is no easy answer to this one, other than to try to find your own balance between blunt honesty and pretence in each and every situation.

- **Be willing to admit when you are wrong!**
  Clients may actually respect you more than you think if you communicate honestly about your mistakes. The authors have been thanked for their efforts in situations where they thought they had made a mess of things. This can only be because mistakes make a worker more of a human being in the client's eyes, and provide a good model of behaviour if they are able to apologize and carry on.

- **Admit to yourself that there will be people with whom you cannot empathize.**
  Empathy requires some kind of common ground or frame of reference which may be impossible to establish, for example with murderers or child abusers. It is important to seek the advice and counsel of colleagues when dealing with such clients.

- **Express your own feelings only when the time is appropriate.**
  There may be occasions when it is entirely appropriate to be honest about your feelings – for example, 'I felt sad when you described your mother'. At other times, for example if you feel sexually attracted to a client, communicating your feelings is clearly unacceptable.

- **Don't trample on people's feelings.**
  Some people are so committed to getting it right logically and analytically that they can fail to appreciate how the other person is feeling. You can disagree without demolishing each other!

- **Non-verbal clients have feelings too.**
  Don't make the mistake of assuming that, because someone does not express themselves overtly, they do not have feelings. If you have a non-verbal client who uses a visual communication system like the ones mentioned on page 34, ensure they have access to a means of communicating their feelings to you.

Angry feelings – conflict management

- **Managing conflict involves knowledge and skills.**
  There are recognized procedures and recognized techniques that work.

- **If you are communicating with a client where a risk of anger or conflict is present, take someone with you.**
  For example, if there is any question of drugs use, or having to give unpleasant messages to someone, do not do this alone. Colleagues should know where you are at all times, and when they expect to hear from you again.

- **Make sure that you are familiar with your organization's safety procedures.**
  If your organization doesn't have guidelines, visit the Suzy Lamplugh Trust website (www.suzylamplugh.org) which has plenty of advice on how to stay safe.

- **View risk assessments as important communications.**
  Some consider risk assessments to be irrelevant paperwork, but remember that each question asked of you has grown out of something which has gone wrong.

- **Reduce your exposure to risk.**
  For example, when there is a concern about violence don't conduct an interview in the kitchen where sharp implements are close at hand.

- **Recognize the common warning signs of anger.**
  These include: repeated succession of the same questions, shouting, replying abruptly or refusing to reply, and rapid breathing.

- **Don't make a bad situation worse.**
  Keep well out of arm's reach; if someone is angry, don't make sustained eye-to-eye contact. Don't corner the person or block their escape route – but do look after your own!

- **Use words that help to defuse the situation.**
  Words that are calculated not to inflame the situation, and that are spoken in a calm, kind but firm way, should help the person who is worked up to become less agitated. Avoiding the use of the words 'you said' and 'you did' will avoid giving your client the impression that they are being blamed.

- **Always remember that, as a professional, you are a target for feelings which are meant for authority figures.**

  The reaction you receive might be to the client's parents or more generally to representations of the state or society. We all adapt in one way or another to messages from our parents, which vary from helpful and supportive to downright dishonest and abusive.

- **In some people such targeting leads to 'under-the-counter' aggression.**

  This is not always easy to recognize, though you may feel vaguely uneasy about a client who seems over-compliant, while making complaints about you to others, being habitually late or making jokes at your expense. When such behaviour happens, it is worth asking yourself, 'What is going on here?', and reflecting on his or her possible motivations.

- **This kind of targeting behaviour can be explained as having its roots in childhood and as a response to feeling powerless.**

- **Someone who has been badly hurt in life may have good cause for feeling angry and upset.**

  However, he or she may have developed ways of punishing you for what others have done, thus gaining sympathy from anyone who will listen and avoiding personal responsibility.

- **Don't think that you're to blame for the client's behaviour.**
  Instead, when he or she does something covertly hostile, use your assertiveness skills to point out the discrepancy between the different messages you are receiving.

- **Whether dealing with covert or overt aggression, stick to the matter at hand and tell the hostile client how these actions make you feel.**
  It is really important to change the 'script' here so that the client does not go on with destructive behaviour. He or she may have gained a certain satisfaction throughout life by playing out angry feelings, but this only leads to being disliked and distrusted.

- **Try to create an atmosphere in which the client will feel comfortable sharing negative feelings openly with you.**
  Tell him or her, 'I know you're angry. Please tell me about it'. Over time, the client will become more honest about feelings and better able to express them.

- **Stay calm.**
  Try speaking to the person as if they are not aggravated. This can be very effective – calmness can be catching!

- **Use your non-verbal communication to calm the situation.**
  Nod your head to assure him or her that you have heard. Maintain eye contact (unless you know that your client is uncomfortable with direct eye contact).

- **Move the conversation to a private area.**
  This is particularly important if others are present. It will help you to communicate without interference. In choosing a location, stay safe (don't choose a spot that is isolated).

- **Check that you are communicating clearly.**
  When the client has finished speaking, ask permission to summarize what they have said to ensure you have understood them correctly. Ask that they do the same after you have communicated to ensure both sides understand one another.

- **Work with the issue, not the person.**
  Don't make things personal. If possible, identify at least one action that can be done by one or both of you.

- **If a dispute cannot be resolved, consider seeking a third party to mediate.**
  This might be a colleague, a friend or a qualified mediator.

- **If things go wrong, walk away.**
  Respond quickly to cues given by your client. If he or she appears to be threatening in any way at all, leave.

- **Finally, always maintain an appropriate wariness.**
  Most assaults happen in entirely unforeseen and unexpected situations – such as being accosted in the corridor of a hostel by a complete stranger who has no relationship with your client.

Handling stress

- **Understand the nature of stress and its effect on communication.**
  Balance the need to maintain a warm, humanitarian and empathic approach to people against the need as a professional to be sufficiently detached and objective. It can be a difficult balance to strike – the process of trying to do so can produce even more stress.

- **Watch out for signs of stress.**
  Only you and people who know you well can assess how far the following common symptoms are normal for you, and how far they are due to temporary or long-term stress: irritability; sarcasm or hostility; losing patience; rushing; being careless or forgetful; use of substances such as alcohol, drugs, cigarettes or medication; difficulty in concentrating; and negative, self-defeating or perfectionist thinking. Think about how disastrous even one item in the list above can be for your work, let alone your life as a whole.

- **Does your character dispose you to stress?**
  Many people choose to work in the helping professions because of personal experiences or traits which themselves render them vulnerable to psychological stress. So it is not just the job which causes stress, it is that 'the character chooses the job'.

- **Seek solutions to stress.**
  There are strategies you can follow: seek consultation and supervision (even if not in a formal capacity within the workplace); some people find yoga, relaxation and

exercise helpful; or talk to people – communicating the problem is the first step in tackling it.

- **Don't ignore stress in a client or colleague.**
  One of the unkindest and least responsible things a person can do is to pretend they have not noticed when someone is quietly 'going under'. If you see someone struggling, summon all you have learned about communication and find a way to persuade them to get help.

- **Be sensitive to hidden stress.**
  Most people have heard of post-traumatic stress disorder (PTSD) resulting from natural disasters, severe accidents or war, but PTSD can occur through a job that someone has done for years. For example, an ambulance driver may have attended a hundred horrible accidents and, apparently unaccountably, break down after the one hundred and first. It is as if the psyche suddenly decides it has had enough.

- **Use helping techniques with clients or colleagues.**
  There are techniques like brief therapy which can be used after a disaster, such as a fire or flood, but they are also relevant when there has been a violent incident. If you work in an environment where there is increased risk of PTSD, ask for training in this.

Using humour

- **Laughter provokes a physical reaction.**
  It is acknowledged that laughter has some beneficial physical effects, for example lowering blood pressure and reducing stress hormones.

- **Humour can help to establish a connection and trust.**
  Clients often view workers who have a sense of humour as helpful, skilful and trustworthy. Humour can be very helpful in taking the heat out of things, and if you have made a mistake but can laugh at yourself, you will show that you are a person who is emotionally intelligent.

- **Don't use humour that will cause offence.**
  This could be intentionally or unintentionally – and includes jokes.

- **Clients can use humour as a negative communication tool.**
  Humour is not always positive. It can be caustic when used to diffuse stress, express frustration or be self-critical.

- **Take particular care when using humour with people of different cultural backgrounds.**
  Even the act of telling a joke or gentle teasing can be viewed as rude within some cultures, particularly where there is a professional person who is seen to be in authority, as opposed to family or friends.

You may feel emotional at times and think that you are up against formidable opposition – it is worth remembering that your client may feel exactly the same!

Chapter 4

Communication in Different Settings

Communication happens in different settings...the place in which you communicate can form a vital ingredient of communication itself!

Where to meet?

- **Consider the setting in which to meet.**
  Is the location convenient and appropriate? Is it busy, private, noisy, secure? Think of your client's preferences; for example, resistant clients might feel all the more defensive if approached in their own home.

- **Wherever you are, be reachable.**
  If people cannot reach you, your skills and knowledge are irrelevant!

- **Ensure that the environment in which you are communicating is inviting and inclusive.**
  If someone has had to struggle to get into the premises to see you, or has had to ask for help because the means of access were inadequate for them, it can have a detrimental effect on a forthcoming session.

- **Choose a comfortable space.**
  Think about the ideal space for your client; some people prefer not to meet in enclosed, busy or very high places.

- **Check the rules if meeting within an institution or organization's building.**
  If you work in an institution (be it a company, hospital, residential home or otherwise), check if there are rules or regulations concerning visitors. Let the client know in advance if he or she will need to sign in.

- **When visiting a client's home, be tactful.**
  Passing comments about decorations or cleanliness may cause offence, and they may have 'house rules' of which you are not aware; for example, the act of not taking your shoes off may ruin your chances of having productive communication. Others may experience feelings of shame and awkwardness which will also spoil a positive, open communication.

- **Think before you enter someone's house.**
  For example, if you are visiting an Asian household, always offer to take off your shoes in the vestibule. You will not know what the household religion or practice is, but many Muslims and Hindus consider the

wearing of outside footwear inside the home or place of worship both unclean and disrespectful. Indeed, it can be a good idea to offer regardless of who you are meeting.

- **Be prepared to cope with having children around in a client's home.**
  Think about whether this will impact on what you need to communicate. If you show that you are happy to have them around, children can take advantage and dominate the proceedings and parents may not rescue the situation for you. If, on the other hand, you ask if a child can be removed from the room, both parent and child might react negatively.

- **Consider any risks associated with the setting.**
  For example, if you are visiting the house of a resistant client, consider any risk associated with doing so, particularly as a helping professional. You may be on your own and isolated from outside help.

- **When visiting households, be alert to safeguarding issues.**
  Safeguarding and child protection is not solely the job of social workers – all health, social care and education professionals have a shared responsibility to ensure that adults and children are being cared for properly. Unless you have professional expertise in this area, don't probe in a way that is likely to raise suspicion or cause offence, but do try to ensure that any worrying observations you make are referred on through the appropriate channels.

- **Communication on trains, planes and automobiles.**

  Many workers will communicate with clients between locations, and this can be a valuable opportunity for useful communication. Many clients reveal things when they are sitting beside you in a car which they would not in a formal setting, face to face, or in an interview setting. Of course, health and safety is paramount in these circumstances, but it is possible to use these opportunities while driving safely.

- **Be alive to creativity when thinking about locations for communication!**

  Settings are more versatile than you think – you just need to be imaginative! For example, you may have the most meaningful conversation with a client in a crowded waiting room, chosen for shouting at the top of your voices – it might be the only environment in which the client feels safe.

  You may not be in control in all settings – stay friendly but never be entirely off-guard. You can always stay in control of yourself!

Chapter 5

Structured Communication

Most communication has a structure...if it doesn't, it will be much less effective in a professional context. Before you communicate, you must first prepare. During the course of the communication, there are then beginnings, middles and ends, with obstacles that can arise between these points. Structured communication can take the form of a single, one-off communication, or a series of formal meetings over a period of weeks or even months.

Preparing yourself first

- **The first, rather comforting, thing to remember is that this is one of the areas you have a lot of control over, unlike resources, buildings and size of workload.**

- **Think about your basic attitude.**
  Your views and attitudes do matter, and will communicate themselves to the client. If you believe

that the client can change for the better, this is more likely to happen – in other words: optimism.

- **Be mindful of any strong beliefs or principles you have – political, secularist, religious or pacifist.**
  They will always be a base for your practice, but it is debatable how far they should be revealed to service users. The authors would always err on the side of extreme caution – even though they are expressing a view here!

- **Remember that every encounter is important.**
  The person you are seeing may be one of many for you today, but for that person, you may be one of very few people they see, and the meeting for them might be crucial. They may also have travelled a long way to see you, at some inconvenience, and have incurred expense that they may not really have been able to afford.

Scene-setting

- **Set up a time, date and place.**
  If you make arrangements by phone, follow up by letter if possible. If you make them at the time when you are seeing the client, given them a written note of the time, date and place. If you make them later, don't forget to phone or write to confirm.

- **Ensure all paperwork you might need in the meeting is available and up to date.**
  It can be very distracting to a client if you have to keep leaving to find forms and leaflets.

- **Consider any other materials you may need and have them ready.**
  You may have watched pilots in films going through their checklists. Well, it is not such a bad idea for you to do the same. Though workers are invariably busy and rushed, it actually saves time if they have a list of what they need available. If you're using technology, check it's working properly before the meeting starts.

Preparing the location

- **Create a welcoming and enabling environment.**
  This might involve using some elements that are similar to those you might have in your own home – a comfy chair or warm lighting – but should also feel relaxed, and not too much like your own territory. Warm, neutral tones and gentle, soothing pictures are best.

- **Consider whether your decorations, pictures and other accessories welcome all groups.**
  Are they images or themes that are more likely to appeal to a particular group or demographic? Will they put all of your clients at ease?

- **Make sure your desk is welcoming.**
  Be honest – does the following describe yours? 'The desk is a jungle. Once there were paths, but they had overgrown as paths do. It was said there were pets (or worse) somewhere in there, living off the tea leaves and old food stores' (Anon). Such a desk may endear you to or alienate you from the public – whichever it is, it gives a message.

- **Check that the venue is accessible to all.**
  Ensure that the venue is accessible to wheelchair users, and that bathroom facilities are appropriate for people with disabilities, etc.

- **Public conveniences should be clean and easy to access.**
  These details will contribute to how a client responds to you. Neglected facilities can communicate the impression of a lack of respect for clients.

- **Refreshments are an important aid to communication.**
  Consider how common it is to meet up for a coffee or lunch, to have a chat over a cup of tea. Food, drink and communication go hand in hand, though this is a fact that is often overlooked and should be thought through.

- **Consider whether or not to offer refreshments.**
  In some institutional settings refreshments may be part of the routine of the day.

- **Plan what refreshments to offer.**
  Be prepared for special dietary requirements and religious considerations – soya milk for vegans, decaffeinated options for tea and coffee, sandwiches with vegetarian/Halal/Kosher options, etc. – and it helps to know what the food contains if asked. Try to avoid providing lavish food or allowing excessive leftovers – doing so may provoke awkward feelings in someone who has little money with which to buy food themselves.

- **Confirm who is paying for refreshments.**
  Check that your workplace has a budget – clients should not feel they have to pay.

- **Consider a structured refreshment break.**
  Within the context of a group meeting, a break can provide an opportunity to revisit comments made within the meeting – perhaps to discuss issues on a one-to-one basis that it was not appropriate to discuss as a group. It might be a subject that others within the group would feel excluded from talking about, or that touches on a sensitive matter.

- **Be cautious about offering alcohol.**

- **Offer alcohol only in very special circumstances.**
  Drinking alcohol can lead to changes in people's personalities – sometimes towards being more relaxed and willing to chat, sometimes towards being more aggressive. You will have workplace guidelines which you will need to abide by, which usually forbid alcohol at all times. However, workplace guidelines may allow

sensible use for appropriate occasions (for example for a birthday or social occasion). However, be aware that some people who are teetotal may disapprove of you choosing to drink in their presence.

- **Take time to relax.**
  At work, take a minute to breathe deeply, close your eyes and picture you and your next client having relaxed communication with a positive outcome.

- **Remember again: every encounter is important!**

  There is as much to do before you see anyone as afterwards, so a revised old adage applies: out of sight but in mind!

Setting the tone

- **Wherever you meet the client you can set the tone by the way you make your entrance.**
  Remember all the tips about facial expression, gestures and posture. Walk towards your client in a welcoming friendly way. People who swagger, walk very quickly, or slouch can be off-putting!

- **Start each contact in a welcoming, encouraging and helpful way.**
  You may think this is stating the obvious, but if you have a string of people to see in a day, you may find your initial good intentions waning after a while.

- **How you greet someone is very important.**
  A greeting expresses shared human ordinariness. More importantly, it can shape the whole contact with

someone, especially if you have not met them before, because impressions take root so quickly and can be hard to shift.

- **Break the ice with a warm approach.**
  Think how you would feel if you were a member of the public confronted by someone who was, for example, like any of the following: cold, abrupt, severe, overbearing, judgemental or self-important.

Introductions

- **Make sure you get names right.**
  This includes knowing before you meet someone what their name is, as well as checking with them how they would like to be addressed. This will, of course, depend on the situation. If it is a formal encounter then surnames will most probably be used. Tell them your name, or wear a label – don't be the anonymous bureaucrat!

- **If you are meeting someone with an unfamiliar name, ask them whether you have pronounced their name correctly.**
  This may feel awkward, but most people will appreciate you taking the time to check. It also gives someone the opportunity to express a preference if, for example, they prefer to be addressed using a shortened form of their full name. If you find it difficult to remember and use people's names – write them down. If working in a group, you could make a seating chart. The more

you address people by their names, the easier it will become!

- **Decide whether or not to shake hands with the person you are meeting.**
  This may seem trivial, but there are some points of which you need to be aware if it is the first time for meeting the person. You may be bound by management guidelines. Even handshakes can be a minefield – a limp handshake by a man can be interpreted in some Western cultures as effete or as a sign of weakness, while in most parts of Africa, a soft handshake is the most common form. There are people who invariably want to shake hands with everyone, and there are those who never want to. Most are somewhere in between.

- **How to shake hands.**
  If you do choose to shake someone's hand, either be pro-active and offer your hand in an unobtrusive way (not thrusting it wholeheartedly at the client) to allow the other person to make a casual handshake, or opt not to offer your hand, but instead watch carefully for the other person to make the first move.

- **Think about your forms of address.**
  People tend to use what they are used to and assume that their way is the right way. You may also instinctively slip into a less formal kind of address when you want to comfort someone. Have you ever liked or disliked the way you were addressed by professionals? The best thing to do is to play it very cautiously: use people's titles and surnames, then ask them how they like to be addressed.

Relationship length

- **The length of a working relationship can have a bearing on how you deal with a client.**
  If you have only one or two meetings then you have very little chance to build up a rapport. With longer term relationships you will naturally have more time to get to know each other and to build up trust. When you meet a client for the first time, you may not know straight away what the length of the relationship is going to be, until you have assessed the situation. The client may not know either.

- **Know how to deal with short-term relationships.**
  Put as much preparation and effort into these as you would for ones which you anticipate going on for much longer. Your client deserves to be cared for just as much as one with whom you work on a longer term basis. And you never know, of course, whether that client will return later, so – as you sow, so shall you reap!

- **Be aware of how to deal with long-term relationships.**
  Good beginnings make for good endings, so starting to build up a good rapport early on will pay dividends later. Read through all the tips in Chapter 1 once again so that you give positive and encouraging messages, non-verbally and verbally.

Setting goals

- **Try to help people translate dreams, hopes and wishes into tangible terms.**
  You can do this without being brusque or dismissive, but it is part of the professional task to help clients to be clear about what they really want, and how to achieve this.

- **Don't get put off by 'goals', 'targets' and 'objectives'.**
  They may convey a hint of 'management speak' but distinguish between words which are unhelpful and ideas which can enhance your practice.

- **Targets and goals are useful motivators, but don't set too many.**
  Make sure goals are achievable, ensure they are agreed upon and clearly understood, and ascertain whether any additional help or support is needed in order to achieve them. It is easy to fall into the trap of setting targets which are too high for someone else.

- **Targets and goals can make things seem achievable.**
  Clients can feel overwhelmed if they are faced with what seem like endless challenges – targets and goals identify particular problems and offer plans to overcome them. They also offer an opportunity to focus.

- **Try out 'task-centred practice'.**
  A 'task' in this context simply means making a problem manageable by breaking it down into small bites which worker and client allocate to each other.

It makes no specific attempt to 'explain' the causes of the problem and assumes that problems are best dealt with by being broken down into specific activities and actions. *All* of the following four steps need to be followed properly in order for it to work:

1. problem exploration
2. deciding on what to do and who is to do it
3. doing the tasks
4. ending and celebrating success.

- **Be conscious that your own goals may differ to those of your client.**
  A tug-of-war is counter-productive. Try to negotiate in a manner that opens up lines of communication. You may, however, reach a point where you have to be firm about what the client needs to do.

- **Review your targets and goals.**
  Be flexible. Your targets and goals may need to be modified in the light of new information. If you do make changes, do so cautiously, and bear in mind the outcome that you really want. It may be that there is a case for abandoning goals or targets which become redundant.

Handling interruptions

- **Don't be the instigator of an interruption.**
  Imagine how you would feel in a reversal of roles. You are the client and the person you have come to see constantly answers phone calls, talks to other

colleagues who want to see her or him, keeps checking a mobile for texts, leaves the room for a while without explanation. You would not be pleased to say the least.

- **Arrange how phone calls and visits from colleagues are to be dealt with when you are in a meeting with your client.**
  You can always respond to messages at a later time. If your organization has an adequate office procedure in place, employees should know how to deal with emergency calls. Make colleagues aware of when and in what circumstances they must not come in and interrupt you. Switch off your mobile, and try to time your loo breaks so that they don't interrupt sessions.

- **Try to keep the interview on track.**
  As you work out with your client how best to respond to their situation, you may have to deal with their wish to digress at times, perhaps in order to avoid difficult issues, or to deal with their nervousness. Steering a meeting back to what you see as the point of it can need skilful handling.

Summarizing

- **Master summarizing: packaging information in easy-to-remember 'chunks' of understanding.**
  The client's narrative can be like the erratic and hard to describe distribution of straw in a field. Summarizing is like the farmer's machine that compacts the straw into a number of bales that are easy to store, measure and comprehend.

- **Remember: people who are anxious, upset or timid may not remember all that has been discussed.**
  For example, some people cannot recall much after an important visit to the doctor. If you are facilitating a meeting or discussion, judge when the session is about to close and give a clear and precise résumé of the main points. If you think it's necessary, or if the client asks for it, give them a handwritten list. If another session is planned, give them a card with a note of the time, date and place.

- **Decide whether or not you would prefer to makes notes as the session proceeds as an aide-mémoire.**
  You can then ask the client if they mind your doing this. If they object, you can either explore why in a non-intrusive way or simply accept their reply. There may, of course, be situations where notes must be taken at the time.

Endings

- **Know the importance of endings.**
  An inability to handle termination may sabotage all that has gone before – be alert to the importance of ending your relationship well. An ending might be the end of a conversation, the end of a meeting or the end of a relationship. All are important in their own way and can be handled well or badly.

- **The end of contact involves a loss.**
  This is true for the worker and the client, even if the interaction has not been experienced as particularly positive. Obviously, a single session or brief contact may not generate strong feelings, but if it makes a big impact a short relationship can be as memorable as communication over several months.

- **Recognize when clients are prolonging the end of a meeting.**
  The client might attempt to do this by developing new problems or re-introducing the old ones. Ask yourself if it is something that can wait – explain that timetables need to be kept to. Some issues will not wait, such as an allegation of abuse.

- **Pay particular attention to how you end a meeting.**
  If it is a one-off, you might be tempted to think it doesn't matter how you end it. Remember that you are dealing with another human being and a caring ending could be an enormous help to them. If you see them again, you will be setting the tone for the next time you meet.

- **Give the person a precise note of any future meeting.**
  Don't just say, 'Well, I'll see you next week at the same time.' If they don't turn up, and you feel it is important that they should have done so, get in touch as soon as you are able to find out what happened. If you feel that their reason is not valid, say something like, 'I'm worried about you. Perhaps we could make another appointment.'

- **Circumstances can magnify the significance of a relationship ending.**
  In situations where loss, grief, anger, guilt or relief are present, the significance of a relationship ending can appear greater.

- **Clients will behave differently to endings.**
  Here are some examples. The client may well opt to drop out as a way of avoiding the sadness of ending what they have found to be helpful contact, without considering the worker's feelings! Others may be angry, and could show this overtly or in other ways, such as turning away from you, not speaking or missing appointments. Apparent anger may mask sadness at leaving. Some clients may rubbish your support; others will show signs of relief.

- **Communicate your own feelings regarding the ending.**
  Rather than feeling rejected, celebrate with your client the positive things which have brought about the end – be sensitive to the fact that the client may have valued the relationship, even if you found it challenging. It is not wrong to be honest about what has been valuable for you, or to express sadness if you feel sad, but don't be negative.

- **When one relationship ends, others begin.**
  Point your client to the prospect of meeting new people or visiting new settings in future.

- **Consider closing ceremonies.**

  This won't be appropriate for many clients, but, for example, if your client is a child you could draw a picture of two people in a car. They set off from one place and travel to another, visiting places which may have meaning, and waiting at the end of the journey is a new start.

- **Think about accepting gifts.**

  Take care if you do go down this route. When receiving gifts you need to consider why the client wants to give you something. Does the organization you work with have rules about receiving presents? Is the present a coded (or not so coded!) message? In answering and acting on these questions, try to keep a balance between humanity and professionalism.

- **Take care with your parting words.**

  In what sort of situations would you feel it would be appropriate to use the following examples: 'Goodbye', 'Cheerio', 'Ta ta', 'See you', 'Have a nice day', 'Bye' and 'So long'. Would you use 'Ta ta' with anyone other than a young child? Would you use 'Have a nice day' to someone who is very troubled?

  There are no absolute recipes for final goodbyes, only the adage: good endings make for future good beginnings.

Chapter 6

Communicating with Different People

People can be lovely, infuriating, kind, cruel, joyful, miserable... The list of attributes is endless. In order to make sense of the many different kinds of people and behaviour out there, you need to recognize some of the differences between them.

Working with men and women

- **Recognize stereotypes about men and women.** Stereotypes prejudice your own attitude towards someone and it is difficult to communicate effectively if you have already decided what someone thinks. Stereotypes include views that men are direct, domineering and authoritative while women are catty, jealous, indecisive and poor drivers. Stereotypes are rarely accurate, and, even when they do point to broad tendencies, they will never be true of all men or women – don't make the mistake of prejudging.

- **Be aware of common variations between genders.**
  For example, past research has suggested that women tend to make more references than men to psychological processes, the home, and emotions in everyday communication, while men use language more for conveying information than description. This means they refer more often than women do to impersonal things, and don't tend to give details of rooms, decorations or atmospheres.

- **Communication can differ in workplaces with different gender balances.**
  If workplaces comprise mainly of men (or women), this can have an effect on how staff communicate. For example, there may be significantly different communication issues for workers in the caring professions where men are in a minority.

- **Do not assume that men or women are better communicators.**
  The fact is that they have different tendencies, but both have complementary things to offer.

Working with children

- **Treat children as people in their own right.**
  They should not be thought of as an extension of yourself, or as 'just kids'.

- **Remember that you can learn a lot from children.**
  They will, of course, learn a lot from you, but sometimes adults forget that the learning is a two-way process.

- **Communicate with children at their level by sitting or kneeling beside them.**
  By physically sitting at their level, you are more likely to be seen as communicating at their level.

- **Play is communication.**
  Play is a form of communication, just as adult behaviour is a form of communication. Sometimes, children can deal with or express uncomfortable feelings through play which they could not do through speech. This might be through drawing, the use of dolls and puppets, and board and card games.

- **Communicate in ways which don't hurt children's essential tenderness.**
  Don't trample over their fears or pour cold water over their imaginative ideas; you risk producing an adult with a hard shell.

- **Don't try to make children be like you.**
  For example, the 'three Fs' – 'Following in father's footsteps' – was a notion very much in favour years ago, but can still influence our relationships with young people, albeit in different ways. Equally, don't try to make them different from you – they may not want to do things you wished you had done but couldn't.

- **Be aware of non-verbal communication when working with children.**
  Adults give children non-verbal messages all the time, whether it be your body language or the actions you take. Think about the ways in which you communicate with a child without speaking.

Working with people of different races and cultures

- **Understand that people of different races and cultures are different.**
  The authors are defining race as a group of people united or classified on the basis of common history, nationality, or geographic distribution, and culture as the customs, values, and traditions that are learned from one's environment. Being different doesn't mean you can't communicate well, but it can make communication a lot harder if you don't recognize and understand this difference.

- **Recognize that your own race and culture is loaded with values.**
  For example, there has been a tendency in the past for white Westerners to assume that they are 'culture neutral', or for whiteness to be seen as a 'default setting' – an absence of race and culture.

- **Take some time to find out more about your clients' customs and conventions.**
  Nobody can be an expert on all cultures, but if you are working a lot with people of a racial or cultural

background with which you are unfamiliar, you'll find it informative and useful to find out more about their lives.

- **Be aware that culture and customs can have very practical implications for communicating well.**
  For example, in some cultures it is not acceptable to send a woman to interview a man, or to send a man to interview a woman. In others, it is considered rude to mention the name of people who have recently died. People share a lot of characteristics, and pride is a common one – nobody likes to 'lose face'. However, what causes offence and damage's someone's pride can differ a great deal.

- **Be sensitive to the fact that language is loaded with political and cultural meaning.**
  For example, the English language contains many words and phrases which give the word 'black' a negative meaning: blacklist, black mark, black market, blackmail, black sheep of the family. It can be difficult to communicate without using a lot of these terms, but be aware of language that has been identified as problematic in the past; 'political correctness' gets a bad press, but it has developed from concerns about real offence caused to minority groups who are often sidelined in mainstream society.

- **If you have to be insensitive, try to do it sensitively!**
  You and your client do not necessarily have a choice about working together, nor about the content of the discussion. However, it makes all the difference

in the world if you know you are going to have to appear insensitive. First of all you may be able to make significant changes, such as taking someone with you with whom your client will feel comfortable. If no change is possible you can convey to him or her that you are sorry that a more appropriate person is not available, and that you need to raise very difficult matters.

- **Be open to making mistakes – it is better to make a mistake than back away.**
  It's a good thing to communicate with a diverse range of people – the more people that communicate and come to know one another, the more that stereotyped, crude, mental perceptions will be replaced by authentic experiences. You can see an example of this in the integrated schools of Northern Ireland, where children from Catholic and Protestant backgrounds have got to know each other as individuals and realize they have more similarities than differences.

- **Don't expect black and minority ethnic colleagues to be the experts on their respective cultures.**
  Do you consider yourself an expert or spokesperson regarding your own ethnic or cultural background? While there are common experiences shared by people who share racial or cultural backgrounds, it can be a mistake to think that, because, for example, a colleague happens to be black, he or she is the ideal person to work with a client who also happens to be black.

- **Recognize the value of ethnic monitoring.**
  Some regard ethnic monitoring as a bureaucratic waste of time. However, it improves communication by taking account of different religious and dietary requirements and making arrangements for translation and interpreting into different languages.

- **Be sensitive when communicating about religion.**
  To do this effectively, you may need assistance from a colleague or advocate if you lack the necessary understanding of a client's faith.

- **Acknowledge the importance of religion in people's lives.**
  Particularly if you work with vulnerable clients – remember that those who are isolated can sometimes find strength and solace in religion.

- **Think about the 'whole person'.**
  There has been a tendency within some professions to think about people only in part; for example, doctors look primarily at the body and how it is working, and mental health professionals have in the past been accused of overlooking the importance of physical exercise on things like depression. People's views, feelings and faith all form an important part of who they are, and in order to communicate well with your client, you need to recognize this.

- **Take care if disclosing your own religion and culture.**
  Think very carefully about disclosing any views, religious or otherwise, which you may hold. Consider

the power you have and how being open about your own views might affect your relationship with your client. What might first seem a helpful way of establishing a connection may appear to the client as an imposition or cause an unexpected reaction.

- **Take advice when faced with an issue about which you have strong views.**
  Cultures and religions differ, and what is part of someone's religion can be seen by others as an abuse of human rights. For example, male circumcision, gay, lesbian and transsexual relationships and arranged marriages are all matters about which people have passionate opinions which differ greatly. If you find yourself in a position with which you are uncomfortable, get informed. Consult with experts when making professional judgements about sensitive matters; for example, speak to the Muslim Council of Britain about arranged marriages.

Working with clients who do not speak English

- **Are you qualified to communicate with someone who does not speak English?**
  Are you in a position to assess someone's need for interpretative services? People may have more English skills than you think, so may want different support according to the situation they are in. They may be happy to speak for themselves on routine matters but want specialist help for important legal or medical issues. Telephone translation services, if available, are

not always appropriate and face-to-face support may be the preferred and more effective option.

- **Consider the benefits and drawbacks of using a professional interpreter with your client.**
  They may prefer family or friends to act as interpreters because they feel more comfortable with them, but the use of family members can be problematic if impartiality is needed, and untrained interpreters can be inaccurate. Conversely, they may value speaking through someone outside of their community if they have concerns about confidentiality. Be aware that your client may prefer an interpreter who is a particular gender or a similar age.

- **If you use an interpreter, remember they are not just translation experts.**
  They also have the ability to convey other important aspects of communication including meaning and emphasis. The same abilities are used where signing and symbolic languages are concerned. You may need to interpret material for them, even when it is in a language they understand; for example from the British Government website www.direct.gov.uk, which is brilliant for a whole range of services.

- **Ensure your translator is trustworthy.**
  If necessary, get permission to tape/video record the interview. Explain that you will be unable to make a written record of what has been said, so you will need to have a tape.

- **It is vitally important to address your communications to the client, not the interpreter.** Almost everyone has heard of the helper who says to the adult client's mother 'Does he take sugar?', but this cliché is easy to forget when you are speaking to someone whose language is substantially different from yours.

Working with disabled and differently-abled people

- **Remember, everyone is born with different advantages and disadvantages. We are all differently-abled. This may seem a naïve thing to say, but it is easy to forget, as exemplified by the insensitive ways in which people are dealt with at times.**

- **Think about the assumptions you and others may be making about a 'disabled' person.**
  'Disability' is a term that can cover everything from mental health problems and learning difficulties to physical difficulties – often, it is the society in which the person lives which disables them. So, try not to think of and describe your client as simply 'disabled' – disabled people are parents, partners, children, employees, artists and sports people, and each of us has our own particular different abilities.

- **Take care with your words.**
  There is not universal agreement on how to describe people with disability – even within the disability

movement there is much disagreement. However, there is plenty of agreement on what *not* to use:

- ▸ 'Afflicted with', 'suffering from', 'victim of' – these convey tragic or negative views about disability which confuse disability with illness and also imply that a disability is a personal burden. Increasingly, disabled people view their disability as a positive rather than a negative experience.

- ▸ 'Handicapped' – this term is dated and inappropriate, conveying images of begging and of disabled people being cap in hand.

- ▸ 'The blind' – describing people in this way is felt by many to depersonalize individuals and neglects the spectrum of impairments, which includes partially sighted people and people with no sight. Instead, use 'people with visual impairments', or 'blind people'.

- ▸ 'Deaf and dumb' – this phrase is demeaning and inaccurate. Use 'a person with a hearing impairment', 'a deaf person', or 'a sign language user'.

- ▸ 'Wheelchair-bound' – physically-disabled people are not tied into their wheelchairs. Use 'wheelchair user' or 'someone who uses a wheelchair'. A wheelchair offers the freedom to move around and is a valuable tool!

- ▸ 'Invalid' – the term literally means not valid.

- ▸ 'Able-bodied' – the preferred term is 'non-disabled'. 'Able-bodied' suggests that all disabilities are physical and that disabled people are incapable, and ignores unseen disabilities.

- **Be aware of insults relating to disability.**
  Some terms used casually in society as insults are not stigmatized in the same way that racist insults are, but be aware that they are equally offensive, particularly to people with mental or physical differences. This includes terms like 'idiot', 'spaz', 'cripple', 'psycho', 'mental' and 'looney'. Even if you don't use these insults, do you challenge others when they do?

- **Remember, disability can be 'hidden'.**
  Some disabilities are immediately obvious, for example when seeing a person in a wheelchair, or with a hearing aid. However there are other disabilities which many people do not know exist, or have never experienced, such as phobias or dyslexia, so don't make assumptions about people's abilities.

- **Don't take our word for it...**
  If you do not have a significant degree of disability yourself, try to get training from those who really know how it feels to be dependent on others in everyday life, either as clients or as carers.

Working with older people

- **Don't be ageist.**
  Ageism involves pre-judging or making assumptions about people simply on the basis of their age – be it young or old. Age discrimination is unlawful in employment, training and education in the UK.

- **Be aware that different generations have different conventions.**

  Conventions of communication common among young people may alienate or be resented by some older people whose attitudes and views were formed in a different environment. For example, someone who grew up in a more formal environment might find embracing or 'air kissing' too intimate when meeting someone who they don't know well. Don't take offence if your friendly action is rejected.

- **Know your limits – you can't be an expert on all cultures and experiences of life.**

  You can't be an expert on all people from all walks of life – each of us is influenced by our family, locality and social class, as well as by the fact that society's standards change over time. However, be aware of your own limitations and try to put yourself in their shoes if you are struggling to communicate with older clients.

- **Don't use 'familiar' forms of address.**

  This could include using first names without permission, and particularly calling elderly people 'sweetie' or 'dear', which paint the elderly as similar to small children.

- **Avoid ageist words and remarks.**

  This applies to people of all ages. For example, 'that old biddy', 'he's a boring old fart', 'kids today…', or 'she's too young to know…'. These, when linked with words like 'only' or 'just' can be even more unkind – for example, 'he's only an old fogey', 'she's just an old lady', or 'he's only a child'.

- **Consider the phrase, 'Have respect for your elders'.**
  In the past, the words '… and betters' were often added at the end. In some societies the 'elders' are looked up to and respected. They may have accumulated a certain wisdom which comes from all their experiences in life. Of course, some of us will know 'elders' who are not so wise!

- **Remember, ageism is very subtle.**
  For older people, the quasi compliment 'You don't look your age' can be offensive, because it implies that you wouldn't look good if you did! Similarly, 'You don't look old enough to have a teenage daughter' demeans the young parent.

Working with people of different sexualities

- **Don't make jokes about people on the basis of their sexuality.**
  Homophobic comments are never acceptable, and neither is using abusive terms such as 'poofs', 'queers' or 'dykes'.

- **Take care to use respectful and appropriate language:**
  - ▶ Heterosexual – someone who is attracted to persons of the opposite sex, emotionally and/or physically.

- ▶ Lesbian – a woman who is attracted to other women, emotionally and/or physically.

- ▶ Bisexual – someone who is attracted to both sexes, emotionally and/or physically.

- ▶ Gay – usually used to describe a man who is emotionally and/or physically attracted to other men, but nowadays increasingly used to describe a lesbian.

- ▶ Homosexual – a word used from the 19th century onwards to describe people who are attracted to persons of the same sex. Its use is in decline because it tends to describe only physical relationships in people's minds, and because it is used detrimentally.

- ▶ TV/transvestite – someone who dresses in clothes usually found on the opposite sex.

- ▶ TS/transsexual – someone who wishes to change, or has changed, sex.

- **Don't make assumptions about the sexuality of your client.**
  Gay, lesbian and transsexual people are some of the most 'invisible' groups in society. You can't assume that someone is heterosexual or homosexual; sexuality is a matter that many choose to keep private. This means, for example, avoiding questions like 'Who is she?' when a male client mentions they are going on a date.

- **Never pressurize anyone to 'come out'.**
  However desirable or useful you may feel 'outing' would be, it must always be the gay person's own choice. For example, if you see a workmate or client leaving a gay club, respect their privacy and keep it to yourself.

Wealth, class and society

- **Don't imagine that you are not affected by social class!**
  Whatever your own background, its advantages and disadvantages travel with you and affect your relationships. While it's often stated that we live in a 'classless society', wealth and social background are actually key parts of a person's identity; it may be true that old class boundaries have become more fluid and ambiguous, but the preconceptions about people of different classes and social backgrounds still persist.

- **Be class-conscious.**
  This turns on its head the usual assumption that it should be ignored. Being clear about your own class position is vitally important, in order to understand that of other people. When considering discrimination, most people say prejudice based on class does not exist today. This makes 'classism' deadly – it is a glass wall which you cannot see, but you can certainly feel it when you have walked into it and hurt yourself.

- **Consider what you associate with the terms 'working class', 'middle class' and 'upper class'.** They are still in common use, but very often there is disagreement about what is meant by them. Some simple definitions might be:

  ▸ working class – the class in society that comprises manual workers and wage-earners

  ▸ middle class – the section of society that comes between the working class and the aristocracy

  ▸ upper class – the people of the highest social rank.

  Classism is alive in most societies, even though the form of social divisions will vary from country to country.

- **Be conscious of class-based language.** You may not feel that this is important, but the words people use can be pointers to people's underlying attitudes to others. Many expressions in common usage, such as 'chav' or 'posho', are used light-heartedly, but they reinforce class stereotypes.

- **Don't make judgements based on someone's accent or language.** People can experience considerable social pressure to change the language they use or the accent they have. This is sometimes due to archaic prejudices that still exist in some quarters about parts of the country being predominantly working class and therefore not suitable for middle-class professional roles. Like so many other aspects, the prejudice which people have against certain accents or use of languages is often unconscious.

- **Class-based prejudice is so broad and diffuse that it is very difficult to define.**
  The few examples given indicate how it can manifest. Are you able to challenge it whenever you recognize it? The more these matters can be openly discussed in the workplace, the more confidence you will have.

This is barely an introduction to 'people' and their wonderful diversity! If nothing else, remember that each person is like all others and unlike all others. Make sure you mind, and they matter.

Chapter 7

Communicating with Self-awareness

The previous section was focused on your clients but it's important to remember that it takes two to communicate. This means knowing yourself – communicate with yourself as well as your client!

Know yourself

- **Your own state of health communicates an important message.**
  It communicates about how you care for yourself. It can also suggest a lack of respect for others if you dress inappropriately or appear not to have made any effort to be presentable to them.

- **If you have any doubts about your hearing, get it checked.**
  It is one of the senses which can deteriorate so gradually over months or years that any changes can go undetected.

- **Know what you like about yourself.**
  Write down five traits which you like to see in others and which you feel are in you as well. Think about how your preferences are reflected in how you communicate or who you prefer to communicate with.

- **Know what you don't like about yourself.**
  People often don't like in others what they don't want to see in themselves. Write down five traits that really bug you when see them in others. Be aware that these traits are your 'hot buttons'.

- **Know your 'communication personality type'.**
  Some communicators are open to everyone and everything, don't make rash judgements, like to help wherever possible, are flexible in the face of change, but may avoid difficult issues that will result in conflict. Other communicators are more frank – they like to know where they are with people, are efficient decision-makers and find solutions efficiently – but may rush in to act without due preparation.

- **Don't base your relationship with your client on a 'need-to-be-liked' basis.**
  Some people are so keen to avoid conflict and promote harmony that they fail to face up to the need for occasional tough thinking and/or talking. Imagine what it might be like if you were on the receiving end of a person who never comes straight out with things and always avoids difficult areas.

- **Beware of communication running too smoothly.**
  This may seem a strange piece of advice. However, in many professions (particularly the helping professions), things rarely progress without conflict or negotiation. It may be that one of the two individuals are avoiding conflict, perhaps because they don't want to prejudice the service they receive from you. If there's anger or disagreement under the surface, it needs to be brought up as it can sabotage your work.

- **Recognize your own needs, and take care of yourself.**
  Do you need saving from yourself? Many wonderful workers wear themselves out, mentally and physically, because they cannot set limits for themselves. They may need to go on working when it would be wise to stop. Then they require a wise and sensitive supervisor or colleague to help them with their boundaries.

- **Self-interest is a powerful motivator.**
  Most people enjoy praise or gratitude from their boss or the clients with whom they work. There is nothing wrong with this, but be aware that indulging your own personal satisfaction or accepting praise doesn't always result in the best outcomes for the client. Avoid accepting gifts, and maintain a friendly but professional distance in communications.

- **Recognize the control and power which underlies professional–client relationships.**
  The feeling of being in control and having power is a very strong incentive for helping people, and it is wise to acknowledge this uncomfortable idea. It may

not be something that you are consciously aware of, and many would prefer to deny it, but as a helper you usually hold a position of power and responsibility. You have the training or expertise which they are accessing, even in a collaborative relationship in which the client is encouraged to be independent.

- **Clients who have been forced into a relationship with you can feel more powerless.**
  For example, if someone has been ordered to have assistance, or has a disability which leaves them with no choice but to receive help, be aware that they may be sensitive and feel extremely disempowered.

- **Be respectful of and sensitive to the knowledge that you have.**
  If you are in the privileged position of having access to personal information about the public, you need to ensure that this information remains private and be wary of disclosing knowledge of this information in communication with that person; for example, a complimentary comment about someone's appearance or home when you know that they have experienced challenges in caring for themselves in the past could be perceived as patronizing.

- **Remember: it is not power in itself which is wrong – it is the abuse of power.**
  The dentist's knowledge-based power is needed to save teeth, and abused children need child protection workers to help them.

- **Finally, bear in mind that you will get to know a client only partially.**
  You cannot be expected to know all that has gone before in people's lives, what experiences have made them the kind of people they are today. Your client will choose what, and what not, to reveal. So, take note that any advice you give on dealing with the situation is based on very little knowledge of him or her, and mostly on your own experience and training.

Personal bias and agendas

- **Are you encountering personal bias or an agenda?**
  An agenda is often an overarching plan or motivation, while a bias is less conscious and doesn't necessarily work towards a particular outcome.

- **Some forms of bias underpinning a person's communication can be positive.**
  These could be, for example, religious creeds advocating care for fellow human beings or personal ethical codes.

- **Agendas can be overt or covert.**
  An example of a covert agenda is a client who engages in manipulative behaviour in order to qualify for a particular service. An overt agenda might be to make you aware of the shortcomings of the service you provide in as many ways as possible.

- **Don't forget people's feelings.**
  These can be a motivating factor behind many agendas.

- **There are often powerful hidden agendas in the workplace team too.**
  There are unwritten rules which people obey without ever discussing them. For example: never sit in the boss's chair in the office; don't eat at your desk; always offer to make a cup of coffee for others when making one for yourself. Some of these agendas are quite innocuous, but living with them can be a bit like swimming in a clear blue sea which has treacherous undercurrents.

Making judgements

- **Recognize when being judgemental is appropriate and inappropriate.**
  For example, an appropriate time is when you are making the best assessment you can about how someone can manage their debts, based on a thorough knowledge of their circumstances. Your expertise in money management is a professional task if you work in an advice centre. An inappropriate judgement is thinking that someone's clothes look too expensive when they have come to you about poverty – this may lead to bias in your assessment. You do not know how the clothes have been acquired; they may have been donated by a wealthy friend.

- **Look closely at the kinds of 'evidence' you use to make a judgement.**
  Judgements are much more the results of experience and background than people might like to think. It is therefore helpful to reflect on the assumptions you have made? Do they relate to the physical appearance of a client? Or the way they speak?

- **Make your initial judgement, examine it, then consider the opposite judgement.**
  This exercise can be a good way to correct bias and encourage well-informed and accurate judgements. For example, if you are inclined to believe someone is in need of help on the basis of how they present themselves, entertain the idea that everyone is likely to present themselves positively, and perhaps are more likely to embroider the truth in order to receive the help they need. This does not mean being cynical, just thoughtful – you can always act on your first impression if you find it to be sound.

- **Be positive.**
  Even if you are making a critical judgement about your client in your mind, send positive messages when you communicate – he or she is more likely to respond in kind.

- **Supposedly 'neutral' official forms and records can communicate judgemental opinions.**
  For example: 'Sarbjit is very demanding' suggests a negative attitude towards her behaviour, whereas 'Sarbjit works hard at gaining the help she needs', gives quite a different impression.

- **Be aware that your client is judging you!**
  He or she may well have had bad experiences with professionals, as well as carrying other emotional luggage. All your efforts to be friendly and present yourself helpfully are played against this background, even if the client greets you politely. He or she makes judgements about you which may be quite unfair, and it can be very difficult to overcome such preconceptions.

Think about your expectations

- **Manage your expectations in communicating with clients.**
  This doesn't mean you can't be positive, just take care to ensure you're not asking others to act beyond their capabilities. Clients may not have the same capacity as you.

- **Remember that your own expectations can differ from those of the client.**
  Clients expect certain standards of service, and these can differ to the standards which you believe to be required. Where expectations differ, try to be positive – it is better to meet high expectations than disappoint clients, and take care not to set low expectations.

Using labels

- **Labels can be good!**
  Labels often get a bad press, and it's true that you shouldn't label people based on prejudice or stereotype,

whether this is categorizing them mentally or describing someone using a reductive label. However, when they are ill, most people feel more comfortable if the doctor can tell them what is wrong. It is true that people fear a frightening illness, and therefore the name of the illness, so doctors used to be reluctant to tell people their actual diagnosis; this was especially true in the case of mental illness. Practice has changed as it has now been recognized that more information decreases anxiety.

- **Clients' carers may be angry if you protect them from professional labels or diagnoses.**
  For example, it is best not to pretend that a school for particular needs, or a care home for people with dementia, is something else. In the end your clients or their carers will find out – being honest from the word go communicates respect.

- **Labels can be 'passports' to obtain services or benefits.**
  If a client does not have a label, it can indicate that he or she is not in need of a service (as professionals tend to use labels to identify types of customer or groups with particular needs). Take the case of people who have 'personality disorders', a vague description which, in the past, did not qualify the individual for any kind of treatment. Now that the diagnosis and symptom recognition of this condition have improved there are established specialist treatment centres, and having your condition recognized and living with an official diagnosis brings benefits.

You have come to this book with two suitcases: one full of clean, fresh, well-loved tools which you have chosen to acquire; the other containing unhelpful 'luggage' from the past. Further training could be valuable in assisting you to discard or enhance anything you found through reading this chapter. Some 'luggage' you may always have to carry, or would wish to. In both 'suitcases' there will be pros and cons from what you bring: everything has two sides.

Chapter 8

Professional Boundaries and Responsibilities

Communication calls for professionalism, which is sometimes revered, often misunderstood, occasionally despised. So what is it, and why does it matter when communicating with clients?

Boundaries

- **Remember that, as a professional, you are not the friend of a client.**
  This can be an unpopular idea, but it is true. It does not mean that you are unfriendly, quite the reverse, but it does mean that you need to acknowledge that you are not on an equal footing with your client. You may have power over resources, or even aspects of their lives, and are paid to have a relationship with them. You are constrained by your professional role, and

cannot be spontaneous in your relationships – even if you are a carer or volunteer.

- **Remember that society makes rules by which you have to abide as a professional, whether you agree with them or not.**
  Contentious examples are keeping someone alive who wishes to die, or withholding money which you think someone should have, but the rules do not allow you to give. It is usually not helpful to tell people that you do not agree with the rules.

- **Keep your professional and private life separate.**
  Having coffee with a client in a public, therefore relatively safe, environment, where the purpose is very definitely to talk over the thing you are meeting about, can be very helpful; an intimate dinner for two 'after work' is definitely not. If you do not respect such boundaries you are making yourself vulnerable to accusation, be it of sexual abuse, fraud, unprofessional conduct or neglect.

- **Balance getting the job done and looking after someone.**
  For example, you may spend twenty minutes out of half an hour listening and offering a handkerchief to someone who is distressed, but it is also necessary to agree some action or plan, or the person may go away dissatisfied. In short, always keep both elements in mind – this process is known professionally as 'task and maintenance'.

- **Keeping boundaries preserves your sanity!**
  You probably know the worker who never switches off, whose meetings with people go on for 'as long as it takes' (common words from this type of colleague). Of course there are crises which disrupt everything, but these may be fewer than you imagine if you are well organized.

- **Maintain time boundaries.**
  Try to keep control of appointments or meetings, and do not let clients delay or distract from what needs discussing.

- **Learn to handle lateness.**
  Sometimes people are late for a good reason, for instance they may have been held up by a traffic jam. The first time this happens with a client, point out that being late shortens the time he or she has with you, as it is unfair to make subsequent clients wait unnecessarily. If a client persists in being late you may have to point out that he or she will have to go to the end of the queue, or that another appointment will have to be made.

- **Have a procedure for dealing with missed appointments.**
  Sometimes people have a valid reason for missing an appointment, such as illness, but they or someone else should let your workplace know why as soon as possible. Some people miss appointments because they are, for instance, afraid, depressed or anxious, or if they can't see the purpose of the contact. In these cases, it is important to try to find out the reason and see if the

client can be helped to avoid missed appointments in future.

- **Be aware of physical boundaries.**
  It's a sad fact of modern life that what may seem to be a normal human response to someone in pain needs to be considered in the context of the client having been abused, or being in fear of it. If you are employed, read your workplace guidance carefully. Guiding principle: 'If in doubt, don't!'

Confidentiality

- **Confidentiality is critical.**
  This is not to say that you will always be in a position to offer absolute confidentiality – if you are not, it is important to communicate to your client what you are obliged to share with other individuals or agencies, even if you think it may have a negative effect on your communication. Check you workplace Code of Practice to establish exactly what your organization's policy is, and ensure you abide by it at all times.

- **If you have obligations to share certain information, give the client a good example as to why you need to do it.**
  For example, most people will accept the principle if they understand that action must be taken if another person could be seriously harmed if information were to remain confidential.

- **Remember that even when you are communicating with an individual, you may also need to communicate with his or her family.**

  If, for example, you are arranging a day trip for a young person, it is good practice to hold a meeting for parents/carers so that they can hear first hand from you about the proposed activities and contingency arrangements.

- **Protect the confidential data you have.**

  Remember that electronic records and communication make it relatively quick and easy for confidential information to be distributed unless protection is put in place – ensure that the data is kept in a safe and secure environment at all times, and that it is made clear who is allowed to access the data and under what circumstances.

- **Good communication involves knowing when and how to withhold information.**

  For example, you need to know the legal circumstances where information may be withheld. These will likely include:

  ▶ information which may be seriously harmful to the client or some other person

  ▶ information which identifies another person who has not agreed to it being passed to the service user

  ▶ information which is restricted by another law, e.g. adoption agency records

  ▶ information given and held for the purposes of preventing or detecting crime, or for prosecuting or apprehending offenders.

Being clear about roles and responsibilities

- **Be clear to clients about your intentions.**
  Lack of communication about roles, responsibilities and expectations will lead clients to become confused, irritated and perhaps even suspicious.

- **To communicate roles, responsibilities and expectations with clarity, consider setting up a contract.**
  This is clearly not appropriate for many professional/client relationships, but is a common device used by those within the helping professions who have an ongoing relationship with a client. It is not necessarily a legal contract, but an agreement which sets out what each person expects from the other. It needs to be mutually agreed – both parties should be encouraged to be open and honest and the client should be asked what he or she expects to receive from the relationship with you.

- **Maintain professional/client contracts properly.**
  If you are to meet regularly, agree on how the meetings will go, how long they will normally last, and what each person would like the outcome to be. Agree on the 'negotiables' and the 'non-negotiables'. Once you have a contract in place, check how it reflects the experience of working with the client. Have you or your client unwittingly added a few unwritten items to the contract which are getting in the way? Expectations may shift, or additions may be made, such as 'I need a cigarette after one hour'.

Communicating in the workplace

- **When working in multi-disciplinary groups, people sometimes do not realize they are playing a different tune as well as a different instrument!** Putting people together in groups representing many disciplines does not necessarily guarantee the development of a shared understanding. The difference in status between some professionals and others, for example between senior medical staff and care assistants, means that the group needs to build up trust and confidence in its members before it is possible to benefit from the contributions of *all*.

- **Simple practical difficulties can sometimes hinder multi-disciplinary working.**
  Actually getting busy people together in one place can be a nightmare. Further work on the relationship between physical space, its utilization, and teamworking is required.

- **Allow for a little 'time wasting' in this context.**
  When a group of strangers meet for a purpose so much time is spent in probing, weighing each other up and avoiding getting down to real business. In the course of these preliminary manoeuvres, basic relationships can be established. Such a seemingly profligate use of time may in reality serve to increase the prospects of success in a multi-disciplinary team.

- **Beware of differences in terminology between agencies.**
  For example the phrase 'care plan' can have numerous meanings. Where possible, inter-agency teams should dedicate time to producing agreed definitions.

- **Role clarification is essential.**
  This means that colleagues must find the time to talk to each other in depth.

- **Professional boundaries can sometimes become blurred in multi-disciplinary teams.**
  A useful exercise to facilitate multi-disciplinary teamwork is to ask everyone to write down jobs which only their work role can do. Stress that this is not about whether they are capable of the particular job, but whether only they, with the required level of training, may do it. For example, only a doctor can prescribe medication for schizophrenia. Usually there is very little which can only be done by the 'experts', and much which can be done by anyone in the team.

- **This can boost professional confidence.**
  Over and over again vital people describe themselves as 'only the caretaker', or 'only the secretary'. If the operating room floor is dirty, the surgeon's skill is likely to be wasted. In a well-functioning multi-disciplinary team, the 'menial' tasks can achieve their true value.

- **Fear of compensation claims inhibits good practice towards supporting choice, but steps can be taken to mitigate complaints and avoid litigation.**

- **Build a culture which allows for risk taking.**
  When things go wrong, the media and society in general are quick to look for someone to blame, but avoiding risk altogether would constrain the choices people can make. To make good choices, people need to understand the consequences and take some responsibility for them.

- **Make friends with conflict.**
  This is particularly important in a multi-disciplinary context, because conflict is probably inevitable at some point, given the lack of resources and that professional jealousies are sometimes exacerbated by stress.

- **Resolving conflict increases security about the team's coping ability.**
  Unresolved conflict is hazardous – resentment and ill-feeling may grow into disunity and disaffection.

- **When disagreements do occur, an agreed process for quick resolution needs to be in place involving appropriate senior management to avoid unnecessary delays in service provision.**

- **Carry out a simple conflict resolving exercise.**
  Ask each person concerned to write down, on their own, under the following headings, what they would like to say to anyone else in the team:

  - Please continue to do the following things you already do, which help my effectiveness.

  - Please do the following things, which would help me to be more effective.

> ▶ Please don't do the following things, or do them less often.

This avoids rambling discussions, and includes an element of valuing each person. By the time everyone has had a turn, a lot of bridge-building may have occurred.

It is interesting that 'professional classes' are often thought of as some of the most highly trained and paid workers, such as solicitors and doctors. The authors believe that people who take on all the above, and more, deserve the same recognition: professionalism is about how to do a job well.

Chapter 9

Rights, Advocacy and Meeting Clients' Needs

As a professional, you may find yourself communicating on behalf of a client – consulting with them and representing their interests. At other times, you will need to act in their best interests without their permission. This is a complex balancing act that requires understanding of both your clients' needs and their rights.

Meeting needs

- **Understand what is meant by a 'need'.**
  Listen for this word in every conversation you have for the rest of the day – you will find many uses, and it is often used when someone actually wants, demands or wishes. It is not appropriate to have a linguistic debate with your client, but in a service-giving context, you and colleagues need(!) to give it a little thought. You

will be required to make a list of what your client needs – see the 'Assessment' section on pages 145–147. As a public servant, you usually cannot meet needs on your own.

- **In the context of working with the public, 'need' might be defined as attention to some aspect of a person's physiological and psychological requirements.**
  In practice this means working towards them feeling safer; feeling freer from threat, harm, pain and discomfort; and realizing more of their potential.

- **Clients' needs may make you feel uncomfortable.**
  This is particularly so when their psychological situation makes them reject people – you and other helpers included! If you accept that they need to do so, because of the way life or other people have treated them, it makes such behaviour easier to accept. You are often the person who has to soften the impact for carers, colleagues and managers.

- **Remember that there is no way that you can meet all needs!**

Understanding rights

- **Understand what is meant by 'rights'.**
  In public service, this means clients can: make choices about their lives, unless they infringe the rights of others; receive the social and health services they need; be informed of available resources; enjoy opportunities

in leisure, education, training and employment; be unique human beings and not suffer discrimination; and make a complaint when something goes wrong.

- **Know your client's rights.**
  Learn your own legal and professional obligations and those of your client. It's important that you are familiar with relevant laws, as you may be in a position where you have to make a decision that could affect his or her rights – for example, balancing the client's right to choose to engage in a risky activity against the right to protection. You also need to know whether or not he or she can refuse the service you offer.

- **Realize that rights are positive.**
  Respecting someone's rights should not be about avoiding getting it wrong – you have an opportunity to make real improvements to people's lives.

- **The relationship between people's needs and rights is complex.**
  Be aware that you will have opinions about what a person 'needs', and these may differ from those the person has the legal 'right' to receive.

- **Every adult has the right to make his or her own decisions.**
  They must be assumed to have capacity to do so unless it is proved otherwise. You must not assume that someone cannot make a decision for him- or herself just because he or she has a particular mental health issue, medical condition or disability. You should make every effort to encourage and support the person to

make the decision, and such work may involve other professionals.

Helping your client to make decisions and choices

- **Understand what is meant by 'choice'.**
  To be able to choose, you need to be capable of making a choice and have sufficient information about the options available to you in order to make an informed choice. Where vulnerable adults are concerned, a worker can easily fall between two stools: either making choices on behalf of the person, acting in his or her own best interest, or attempting to offer choices which may be beyond the person's ability to comprehend or capacity to make a choice.

- **Decision making is not easy.**
  Making a good decision is a process that involves knowledge, skill and judgement – people's skills may need some enhancing – perhaps including yours! Most people rely on whatever they have done before when needing to decide. These 'strategies' to aid decision making vary from the very helpful, such as finding out lots of information about his or her situation, to the more unhelpful, like resorting to drink or illegal drugs as a form of support to enable decision making. People sometimes take the 'sleeping on it' option, hoping that the decision will somehow make itself. Don't assume that what helps you will help the client.

- **Clients are less likely to rush if a professional is available to consult.**
  They are more likely to use the opportunity of having a sounding board, rather than rush into unconstructive action, particularly if there is a degree of distress or fear associated with making the decision.

- **Recognize the usefulness of support networks in helping clients to make a decision.**
  You may want to enlist the support of others, such as family, a team or a network. Many family reconciliations take place as a result of the support process, and, perhaps for the first time, your client may actually gain comfort from association with people who have similar problems. It may be that someone who has helped before can do so again. Whether enlisting the help of family or other professionals, ensure the outcome chosen has consistent support from all – sometimes called 'singing from the same hymn sheet'!

- **Remember that the client is the person who has to take responsibility for the outcome.**
  It is hardly fair if he or she has had no say in the decision or has been pushed into it!

- **Remember that clients may not be ready to make a decision or to take action.**
  Doing nothing, other than affirming and providing information, *is* an option. Even talking about possible decisions may plant a seed for action in the future. Work to get an idea of the client's understanding of and attitude towards making the decision.

Being an advocate

- **Know about advocacy and advocates.**
  Advocating is the process of representing and speaking up for a client, sometimes on a client's behalf. You can do advocacy work and develop skills without being a professional advocate. There are also professional advocates with whom you may be required to work. Professional advocates are independent. They are not connected to the carers or the services which are involved in supporting the person. They will work one to one with the client to develop his or her confidence wherever possible, and will try to ensure that the person feels as empowered as possible to take control of his or her own life.

- **Recognize the different kinds of professional advocate.**
  There are two main types of advocate:
  1. advocates who support those clients who want to and are able to raise their own concerns
  2. advocates who aim to empower and support those clients with more complex needs, who may not be able to speak for themselves.

- **Families and carers can also appreciate advocacy.**
  Emotions can run high and interests may conflict, so you need a clear perspective on rights and needs, while supporting everyone.

- **In all work with clients and their families – whether assisting decision making or advocacy**

work – always be honest about what you can and cannot do.
This is not as easy is it might sound. Doing so involves knowing or being willing to find out if, where, when and how information or services can be provided – a lot of patient negotiating.

- **Your responsibility to advocate for your client does not diminish your professional responsibilities.**
  You may sometimes be required to carry out an action with which your client disagrees strongly. It sometimes helps to explain that you have needs too – in order to help them – and that you need to satisfy the demands of your organization.

Practice tip: everyone has the same rights but different needs.

Chapter 10

Communication and Procedures

Understanding procedures is one thing – communicating them well is another...

Know the rules

- **To be effective, you must know what your organization's formal procedures are.**
  Putting in writing what you are expected to do, and how you will do it, helps to raise standards by ensuring that everyone works to an agreed level. If you are a volunteer, or an informal carer, it is still helpful to know what the organizational procedures are. After all, you are the one who has to communicate them to the client.

- **If you think that procedures are restrictive, remember that they are often formed in response to something that went wrong.**
  This applies particularly to risk assessments. If you find form-filling time-consuming, remember that previous

tragedies have happened partly because there were no safety nets and due to poor record-keeping.

- **Know that procedures protect.**
  You operate in an increasingly litigious age. Although you may not wish to start from a defensive position, you are always at risk of being blamed if anything does go awry. So, to protect yourself, you do need to be able to say 'I followed procedures'.

- **Find the right words to describe procedures to clients.**
  Avoid formality and the language of procedure when communicating with clients, even if you are communicating about them. Saying 'It's procedures, I'm afraid' doesn't mean anything to your client, and disassociates you from why they are in place. Instead, explain in plain English why you need to act as you do, and what the benefit will be.

- **Formal does not need to be complicated.**
  Here is a simple way to lay out a plan for a professional task in a nutshell: What needs to be done? Who is going to do it? When is it going to be done? How is it to be done? Has it been done? At the end of the day, remember that formal procedure makes action more straightforward.

- **Finally, go the extra mile to ensure that clients are clear about the results of their transaction with you.**
  At the end of a hard day it can seem like a million miles, but that extra letter or phone call to confirm arrangements may prove to be absolutely crucial.

Assessment

- **Assessment is not just for social workers.**
  It is part of a professional toolbox for all workers with people, so that they and their clients can find out what needs doing and match this with what is available. In order to assess well, you need to be a skilled communicator.

- **Assessing needs and requirements is a really skilled job.**
  You are often called upon in a very short time to:

  - build a relationship with the person you are working with

  - learn to understand the way that person communicates

  - spend time with the person finding out what is important to him or her

  - get permission, where possible, from the person to talk to other people about them

  - put forward the wishes and views of the person you are working with

  - provide information in plain language

  - support the person to make informed choices

  - attend meetings, write letters, and make telephone calls

  - enable negotiation and resolution of conflict to take place

> ▸ handle personal information in line with legislation and with due regard to confidentiality

> ▸ investigate and resolve complaints in line with the complaints procedure

> ▸ take cultural, religious and lifestyle needs into account

> ▸ assess eligibility for services according to your organization's policy.

- **Don't underestimate the client's own strengths.**
  There is often a distressing gap between what is needed to make an assessment and what is available. Critical to the assessment process, but often overlooked, is people's resilience. If you can communicate sincerely and honestly about strengths as well as needs, you may overcome some of the deficiencies in various services.

- **Use a life road map for assessment.**
  This is fairly simple to construct. The worker asks the client to draw a 'road' on a large piece of paper. The road will have a number of bends and turns in it. The worker then asks the client to write a brief comment about an event in his or her life that he or she perceives as significant at each turn and twist in the road. As events are being written onto the road, the worker and client may talk about them and weigh up together the significance of each. This will help to identify further areas for exploration and clarify other points.

- **Finding the fastest solution is not necessarily the best one.**
  In spite of the demands placed on workers, clients do appreciate someone taking time and trouble over them. Tell them *what* you have to do, and *why*.

Recording and reporting

- **Remember the importance of keeping records.**
  Recording your work is one of the differences between 'skilled helping', and other kinds of intervention. As a friend, you would normally not make a note about a conversation, but as a professional you are usually required to keep official records of some kind.

- **Maintain good practice when keeping records.**
  Records may be relied upon as evidence in court, and must be accurate, to the point, up to date, relevant, easy to read (in plain English), easily understood by your client, and filed very soon after the event.

- **Bear in mind that your record will be referred back to.**
  Some situations may be sorted out satisfactorily in one encounter, but for others there will be a need to check out whether the plans, procedures and tasks set for a person to work on after a session have been implemented.

- **Remember that your records are influenced by your own background and outlook.**
  Read your colleagues' written records to see if you note any significant changes in style and emphasis.

- **Share your written records with clients.**
  It can be an excellent way to establish rapport. You might read them together as part of a review, or to discuss what each party thinks has happened within a meeting.

- **Clients usually have a right of access to any document that concerns them.**
  Clients need an opportunity to study information obtained from relevant sources and to ask for any necessary explanations.

Background checks and safeguarding

- **Checking is something which you neglect at your peril.**
  Background checks form a normal part of work in the helping professions – whether it be the background and past actions of clients or of colleagues. While background checks can be unpopular, remember that they are there to keep you and your clients safe.

- **Carry out a background check with the right attitude.**
  Nobody likes to prejudge, and clients can feel interrogated when someone carries out a background check on them before they have even met, but it can be reassuring that the person working with them knows how they have come to be in their current position. It

can be much more embarrassing and difficult to have to tell the whole story again to someone.

- **Avoid confrontation by referring to the law.**
  Colleagues or clients may take offence at the thought that they are not to be trusted. If this happens, simply refer to the rules and don't allow yourself to be pressured into backing down – refer to the 'Challenging' section on pages 57–59 and the 'Angry feelings – conflict management' section on pages 69–73. All staff and volunteers who have contact with children and vulnerable people must have a check of their records through the Criminal Records Bureau (CRB). Before this has been done, they must never be left alone with the client.

- **Don't be intimidated into not challenging.**
  Even if someone looks official, ensure that all unfamiliar individuals showing interest are appropriately challenged, for example if someone appears to be lost in the building. You can offer assistance without being confrontational.

- **Carry out a basic risk assessment of any places you intend to visit.**
  It is important to highlight vulnerable areas of rooms/centres/homes, such as concealed entrances or unsupervised areas. This again requires sensitive handling, as your procedures may seem like implied criticism of managers' much loved and cared for establishments.

Dealing with abuse

- **Develop a sensitivity to abuse.**
  This is one aspect of reading non-verbal or obscure communication. Experienced workers often develop a 'feeling that all is not well'. While not evidence, such intuitive signals may lead you to keep your 'inner eye' open.

- **Know the signs of an abusive relationship.**
  Some include exhibiting fear of a partner or parent; unwanted touching; money or property taken without consent or under pressure; not being cared for properly; denial of privacy, choice or social contact; being left in unsafe situations or without medical attention; constantly being 'put down', insulted, sworn at or humiliated; children growing up in a home where there is domestic violence; or children living with parents or carers involved in serious drug or alcohol abuse.

- **Never try to deal with suspicions of abuse by yourself.**
  This is an area where you must be aware of your workplace procedures. This book can only point to basic principles.

- **Report any suspected abuse – financial, emotional, physical or sexual – without delay.**
  Take that first step quickly, as it is the most difficult one. It may seem harsh, or you may be frightened about opening up a whole can of worms – what will the implications be? If you act and are mistaken,

any damage to your relationship with the client can be repaired; however, if you are right but don't take swift action, the damage to another person may be irreparable.

Responding to complaints

- **Regard feedback as valuable and take notice.**
  Whether positive or negative, it can help to make improvements to your own work and that of the service you provide.

- **Make sure you know what your organization's complaints procedures are.**
  Most go something like this:

  1. Client is encouraged to try to sort out the matter with the staff member concerned, except in cases of abuse where it is important that a manager is brought in at an early stage.

  2. Client contacts the Complaints, Comments and Representations Unit.

  3. Client and an appointed officer work together to resolve the problem.

  4. If the complaint is still unresolved there will be an investigation by a senior officer who has no direct links with the team or individual being complained about, followed by a panel which makes a decision and informs the client.

- **If you are responding to a complaint, make sure you have all the information before you do so.**
  This can be difficult at times if someone is economical with the truth when presenting their case – more facts may emerge during the interview, and it can be difficult to respond to these on the spot. Be prepared to revise your opinions and judgements in the light of the information available to you.

- **Don't make hasty judgements.**
  This can be very tempting if you are busy and have a lot of people to see. However, each complaint deserves a proper investigation, and you must balance as fairly as possible the needs of your organization and those of your client. A hasty judgement which refuses a person's claim, which may with adequate investigation have turned out to be genuine, could result in their taking the matter further and higher.

- **If a complaint against you is turned down and you have to continue to work with the client, do so with courtesy and respect.**
  Aggressive, hostile or threatening behaviour tends to beget the same from the person on the receiving end. There will be occasions when you will have to disagree with a complainant, and you must try to keep your composure, and not fly off the handle. Think how you would feel if the roles were reversed – how would you like to be dealt with if your complaint were turned down?

- **Protect yourself following a complaint.**
  Keep accurate records of discussions – such documentation will be critical in order to protect you and the client, as well as the provider of care in the event of any complaints or litigation.

- **Remember, in a supporting role you have a responsibility for helping people who need to complain to do so.**
  This stands even if it means enabling them to lodge a complaint against you.

Supervision

- **Make use of any supervision available to you to support your communication with clients.**
  This might be consultation with peers or a senior member of staff – it is always useful to have feedback. Supervision is not just about 'checking up'. It provides an opportunity to acknowledge work well done and to explore your development needs.

- **Consider using peer supervision groups.**
  These work best with six to eight members who are committed to meeting regularly and act to challenge and support each other.

- **Even trained and experienced practitioners benefit from supervision.**
  It can be a form of support to help combat stress as well as to develop your practice.

- **Supervision protects clients by involving an impartial third party.**
  This helps to reduce the risk of serious oversight and aids reflection on the workers' own feelings, thoughts, behaviour and general approach with the clients.

Reflecting on practice and developing your communication

- **Seeking feedback from clients and colleagues can be a valuable way of learning and developing as a professional communicator.**

- **Know the communication skills needed to evaluate successfully.**
  These include collecting information for planning services, monitoring where things have gone wrong to avoid future problems, proving the value of what you are doing and reporting back to those with an interest in your project (whether they be participants, funders, or the local community).

- **Listen to what your clients feed back.**
  You may find a consistency about what they say which is extremely valuable, if not always comfortable.

- **Experiment with different ways to get feedback from clients.**
  They should be asked if they are willing to give their views and time must be taken to explain the reason for their involvement.

- **Use methods appropriate to the client's preferences and needs.**
  Questions used should be in plain English or various languages and may be asked verbally or in writing, depending on individual circumstances. For children, people with learning difficulties, and those who do not use words, games designed for evaluation can be used; for example, using smiley faces or number cards as 'rating' measures.

- **Be aware that agendas can underlie feedback.**
  For example, clients may be influenced by the fact that they do not wish to offend, in case they prejudice professionals against them.

- **Gain feedback from colleagues as well as clients.**
  This form of feedback derives from colleagues meeting with one another and talking over difficult situations involving colleagues or clients.

- **If you are running a series of meetings with a client, you can incorporate an evaluation within the structure of these meetings.**
  Usually an evaluation will come before the last session. This allows for difficult issues to be dealt with as far as possible, gives participants a chance to avoid taking away burdensome emotional luggage, and is an opportunity for acquiring celebratory feedback which could make the journey easier.

Appraisal

- Supervision goes hand in hand with a personal appraisal and evaluation system.

- If you find this idea threatening, remember that the purpose of appraisal is to:
  - review your achievements
  - discuss any difficulties you may have had
  - consider any training needs
  - make career development plans.

- Appraisals should take place on at least a yearly basis.

- You have a chance to prepare for the appraisal meeting by thinking about your work and completing a pro-forma.

- The pro-forma, which forms the appraisal meeting agenda, includes:
  - your main achievements since last appraisal
  - any difficulties you have had which have affected your performance
  - any targets you think you can achieve by your next appraisal
  - what you think you need from the organization to help you reach these targets

- ▶ any specific areas where training would help you improve your performance
- ▶ any other issues you would like to raise.

• **It is obvious that the appraiser (who may be you if you carry any kind of supervisory role) needs excellent communication skills in order to carry out an appraisal effectively. In particular, he or she should:**

- ▶ put you at your ease
- ▶ start on a positive note by mentioning any aspects of your work which are praiseworthy
- ▶ ask you to talk through your own appraisal of your work
- ▶ add his or her views about your performance
- ▶ review your long-term career plans and training needs
- ▶ discuss and agree a new set of targets
- ▶ agree, summarize and record the content of the meeting.

• **Note how close these skills are to the ones you are expected to possess for your work with clients.**

• **So, appraisers, remember that you are also being appraised by your supervisees!**

Epilogue

A woman who had had a high-powered job was once applying for employment after having had children. She felt de-skilled and lacking in confidence. Then she sat down and made a list of the skills she had used in running a home and caring for children. She spoke of these in the interview. She got the job!

This story underlines the fact that this kind of skill – communicating with people – is often unrecognized or taken for granted. If, in reading the book, you have found some of the tips obvious, this probably means that you are more expert than you think. However, their inclusion is prompted by the authors' amazement that 'obvious' instructions, advice and ideas are not put into practice more often. Don't forget to include them in making a list of your skills and experience!

We will never get it all right… We will never stop trying.